World Future

Human Immortality and Electronic Civilization (v.5)

(That is part of Collection articles, interviews, discussions about people Immortality and Human Future translated from same book in Russian. The fiftieth edition)

Alexander Bolonkin

Intellectual artificial man continues your life

Lulu, USA 2019

Title: **Human Immortality and Electronic Civilization (v.5)**
Author: **Alexander Bolonkin** <abolonkin@gmail.com>
USBN 978-0-359-57711-8

Book is described the arrangement of the Immortality. This is the scientific prediction of the non-biological (electronic) civilization and immortality of human being. Such a prognosis is predicated upon a new law, discovered by the author, for the development of complex systems. According to this law, every self-copying system tends to be more complex than the previous system, provided that all external conditions remain the same. The consequences are disastrous: humanity will be replaced by a new civilization created by intellectual robots (which the author refers to as "E-humans" and "E-beings"), These creatures, whose intellectual and mechanical abilities will far exceed those of man, will require neither food nor oxygen to sustain their existence. They may have the emotion. Capable of developing science, technology and their own intellectual abilities thousands of times faster than humans can, they will, in essence, be eternal.

Copyright @ 2019 by author.
Published LULU in USA, www.lulu.com

Abstract

Immortality is the most cherished dream and the biggest wish of any person. In book the author shows that the problem of immortality can be solved only by changing the biological human into an artificial form. Such an immortal person made of chips and super-solid material (the E-man, as was called in earlier author articles and book) will have incredible advantages in comparison to conventional people. An E-man will need no food, no dwelling, no air, no sleep, no rest, and no ecologically pure environment. His brain will work from radio-isotopic batteries (which will work for decades) and muscles that will work on small nuclear engines. Such a being will be able to travel into space and walk on the sea floor with no aqualungs. He will change his face and figure. He will have super-human strength and communicate easily over long distances to gain vast amounts of knowledge in seconds (by re-writing his brain). His mental abilities and capacities will increase millions of times. It will be possible for such a person to travel huge distances at the speed of light. The information of one person like this could be transported to other planets with a laser beam and then placed in a new body.

This is the popular book about the development of new technologies in 21st century and future of human race. Author shows that a human soul is only the information in a person head. He offers new unique method for re-writing the main brain information in chips without any damage of human brain.

This is the scientific prediction of the non-biological (electronic) civilization and immortality of human being. Such a prognosis is predicated upon a new law, discovered by the author, for the development of complex systems. According to this law, every self-copying system tends to be more complex than the previous system, provided that all external conditions remain the same. The consequences are disastrous: humanity will be replaced by a new civilization created by intellectual robots (which the author refers to as "E-humans" and "E-beings"), These creatures, whose intellectual and mechanical abilities will far exceed those of man, will require neither food nor oxygen to sustain their existence. They will be devoid of emotion. Capable of developing science, technology and their own intellectual abilities thousands of times faster than humans can, they will, in essence, be eternal.

Key words:, Immortality, future of humanity, 21st Century, non-biological civilization, computer.

Contents:

Short Biography of Dr. Alexander Bolonkin (2007)

A. Bolonkin was born in c. Perm (Russia). When he was young, he had National and World records in aviation modelling and was awarded with gold and silver medals. He graduated with awards from *Aviation Collage*, Faculty of Aviation Engines, (**B.S.**)(USSR); *Kazan Aviation Institute*, Faculty of Aircraft Design, (**M.S.**); *Kiev University*, Faculty of Mathematics, (**M.S.**); *Moscow Aviation Institute,* Rocket Department, dissertation *"Optimal Trajectories of Multistate Rockets"* (**Ph.D., Dr. Sci.**); *Leningrad Polytechnic University*, Aerospace Engineering Department, dissertation *"New Methods of Optimization and their Applications"* (**Post-Doctoral Degree in the former USSR**).

He worked in Soviet aviation, rocket and Space industries and lectured in main Soviet University about 15 years. In particularity, in Kiev Aircraft State Design Bureau headed by **O. Antonov**, Bolonkin took part in design of aircraft AN-8 through AN-225 (*Engineer-Senior Engineer-Chairman of Department*); in Rocket engine Construction Bureau headed by Academician V.P. Glushko, Bolonkin was *Chairman of Reliability Department* and took part in design of rocket engines for main strategic rockets of the USSR; in TsAGI (central Aero-Hydrodynamic Research Institute) A. Bolonkin was a *scientific researcher.*

He lectured as a *professor* and worked as a Project Director in **Moscow Aviation Institute, Moscow Aviation Technological Institute, Bauman Highest Technical University**, Technological Institute, He contacted with Construction Bureaus of Tupolev, Yakovlev, Mikoyan, Ilushin, Sykhoy, with all main aviation, rocket and space research and design Centers of the USSR. He had many awards in the Soviet Union.

In 1988, Alexander Bolonkin arrived as a political refuge in the USA and became American citizen in 1994. He worked as a mathematician in Shearson Lehman Hutton (American Express), N.Y., (Research, computation, programming, Optimal portfolio of securities), a Senior Researcher in Courant Institute of Mathematical Sciences of New York University; two years as a Senior Research Associate in Wright Laboratory, Flight Dynamic Directorate (Dayton, Ohio), (it is the main Laboratory of the USA Air Force with over 20,000 scientists); as a professor in New Jersey Institute of Technology, Computer and Information Department. He worked as an expert of Association Engineers and Scientists in N.Y.C. (Estimation of new ideas, projects, patents. Consulting).

He worked two years as a Senior Research Associate in the NASA (Dryden Flight Research Center) in California, Edwards and two years as Senior Researcher in Eglin USA Air Force Base (Florida). Now Dr. Bolonkin lectures in New Jersey Institute of Technology.

For last four years alone, A. Bolonkin published more 35 scientific articles and books in the USA and a lot of articles in Russia-American press about scientific problems. He took part in three World Space Congress (1992, 1994, 1996), in World Aviation Congress (Los-Angeles, 1998, 1999) and more tens National Scientific Conferences in the USA. In particularly, he published monograph *"Development of Soviet pocket engines for Strategic Missiles"*, Delphic Ass., USA, 1991, 133 p., and large Chapter *"Aviation, motor, and Space Designs"* in book **"Development Technology in the Soviet Union"**, pp.32-80, Delphic Ass., USA, 1990; book **"Non-Rocket Space Launch and Flight"**, by A. Bolonkin, Elsevier, 2006, 488 ps.; chapters: *Space Towers, Cable Anti-Gravitator, Electrostatic Levitation and Artificial Gravity* in collection **"Macro Engineering: A Challenge for the Future"**, edited by V. Badesky, R.B. Cathcart and R.D. Schuilling, Springer, 2006; book **"New Concepts, Ideas, Innovations in Aerospace and Technology"**, by A. Bolonkin, Nova, 2007 and others.

Alexander Bolonkin is the author of more 140 scientific articles and books and 16 inventions.

B. Kruglyak, Ph.D.

Chapter 1

The Twenty - First Century: The Advent of the Non-Biological Civilization (1993)

Summary

The author writes about the danger which threatens humanity in the near future, approximately 20-30 years from now. This is not a worldwide nuclear war, a collision with comets, AIDS or some other ghastly disease that we may not even know may be lurking out there (think of the recent Ebola scare or the so-called "flesh-eating" virus). In each of these cases there is still hope that somebody will be saved and that life will be born anew, albeit in a misshapen form and in an inferior stage of development. But we cannot hope for salvation in the author's grim scenario. The danger he writes of will destroy all humanity and all biological life on Earth -- and there is nothing we can do to prevent this! Should we be frightened by this? Is it good or evil for human civilization? Will people awake to find they are only a small step away from the Supreme Intellect, or in other words, to God? And what will be after us?

These and other questions are discussed in this chapter.

The Law of Increasing Complexity

The World, Nature, Techniques consist of biological or technical systems. These systems have a different rate (degree) of complexity. The main distinction biological systems from technical systems is the ability for unlimited self-propagation, or reproduction.

Any system which has possesses this attribute becomes viable, stable, and fills all possible space. It will continue to exist as long as the conditions which gave birth to them cease to change greatly.

Here there is no violation of the entropy law. When the complexity of one system increases, the complexity of other systems decreases.

A more complicated system can be created by using less complicated systems as a base for its development. Such a complex system is a system of the secondary degree of complexity. It increases its own complexity by decreasing the rate of complexity of inferior systems or by destroying them altogether.

Using low degree systems as a base, systems of the second, third, fourth, fifth et cetera levels can be created. Some of the lower levels may not survive and disappear. This, however, is of no great concern because these lower level systems already fulfilled their historical mission by spawning ever more complicated levels.

A necessary condition for the existence of complicated level systems is the ability of inferior systems to reproduce and give birth to other systems, and to do it without limits before they fill in an admissible space and reach their maximum physical boundaries.

This I assert to be the Fundamental Base Law of Nature, the very purpose for the existence of Nature. This **Law** can be stated as follows:

The Law of increasing complexity of self-coping systems.

The history of life on Earth confirms this law. Following the law of probability, organic molecules appeared in prehistoric time when the external conditions for their existence were favorable. Those molecules which had the ability to reproduce filled in the available space. Using them as a base, microorganisms then appeared. These could absorb the organic and inorganic substances and reproduce themselves. Microorganisms as a base in turn gave rise to vegetation which provided food for the next level of animals, which in turn spawned the beasts of prey who devoured other animals. At the present time Man is at the acme top of this pyramid. The human brain can outperform the brains of other animals including man's nearest ancestors, the apes. Man began to use for its development all previous levels as well as the zero level-- lifeless nature.

The Birth of the Electronic Civilization

Only Man's brain has the ability to think abstractly and to make mechanical devices and machines which increase productivity. Such attributes allow us to confirm that humanity is the next level of the biological world. But in our headlong progress during the current century (aviation, space, nuclear energy, and so on.), we have failed to notice that Man has also given birth to the new top level of complex systems or of reasonable civilization, which is based on an electronic not biological basis. I am speaking of electronic computers. The first models were designed at the end of the 1940s.

In the past fifty years, roughly four generations, the field of electronics has developed at an extremely fast pace. The first generation of computers were based on electronic tubes, the second generation on transistors, the third generation on chips, and the fourth generation on very tiny chips which contain thousands and tens of thousands of microelements. The first computers had a speed of computation less then 100 operations per second and a memory of less than one thousand bits (a bit is the simplest unit of information, which contains 0 or 1). For example, the first electronic calculator (SSEC), designed by IBM in 1948, had 23,000 relays, 13,000 vacuum tubes and the capacity to make one multiplication per second.

At the present time the speed of the fourth generation of computers which uses integrated circuits is approximately a billion operations per second. For example, the American computer Cray J90 has up to 3.2 gigaflops of power and 4 gigabytes of memory (one byte equals eight bits). The memory of a laser (compact) disk has several billion bits. Every 3-5 years computer speed and memory doubles, while at the same time their size is halved. Over the past fifty years computer speed and memory have increased a million times. Whereas the first computer required a room 100 square meters (1000 sq. feet) in size, the modern notebook computer is carried in a case. The CPU (Central Processing Unit) chip of a personal computer is no larger than a fingernail and is capable of making more 100 million operations per second!

The fifth generation of computers is just ahead. These new computers will be based on new light principles which guarantees a quantum leap in computer speed. Scientists in all the industrialized countries of the world are already hard at work on the new light computer.

Since the 1950s the new branches of science in artificial intelligence and robot technology have made significant strides and great successes have been recorded. Robots, controlled by computers, can recognize some things, even speech. They can also perform corrective motion and make some complex works, including the creation of a large number of various programs and databases for scientists, stockbrokers, mathematicians, managers, designers, children etc.

Sometimes these programs run smoothly, solving many problems that people cannot. For example, programs have been devised that find and prove new theorems of mathematical logic and there are modern chess programs available that can defeat grandmasters.

These fields of artificial intelligence and robot technology, based on computers, are developing very rapidly, just like computers. Their rate of success depends greatly on computer speed and memory. The production of industrial robots is also progressing quickly. "Intellectual" chips are used in everything from cars to washing machines. Now many experts cannot definite they talk with computer programs or real people.

If the progress of electronics and computers continues at the same rate (and we do not foresee anything which can decrease it), then in the end of the current century computers will have the capabilities of the human brain. The same path, which took biological humanity tens of million of years to complete, will be covered by computers in just one-and-a-half or two centuries.

"So what ?"

- say some readers. "This is great! We get excellent robot servants who will be free from man's desires and emotions. They won't ask for raises, food, shelter, entertainment, or commodities; they don't have religions, national desires, or prejudices. They don't make wars and kill one another. They will think only about work and service to humanity!"

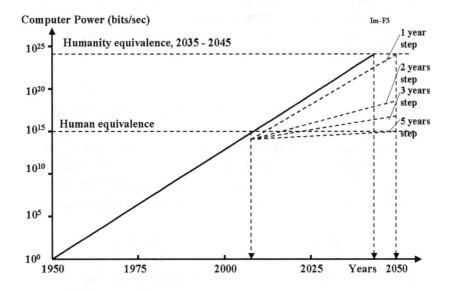

Fig. 1-1. Rise of Power of Supercomputers. The real curve from 1950 to 2005. Extrapolation is after 2005. The step means period of time, when the computer power increases in two times. The computer power will approximately reach human equivalence (HEC) in 2010. Super computer will reach humanity equivalence in 2040 or later.

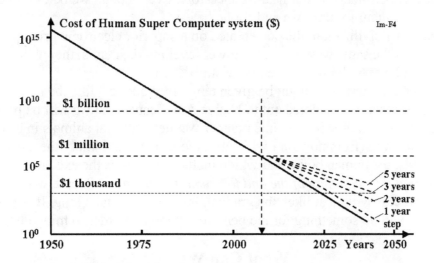

Fig. 1-2. Price of Human Equivalent Super (HEC) computer. The real curve is from 1950 throw 2005. Extrapolation is after 2005. The step means period of time when the computer power increases in two times. HEC will be acceptable for immortality of the most people in industrial countries after 2040.

This is a fundamental error. The development of the electronic brain does not stop at the human level. The electronic brain will continue to improve itself. This progress will proceed millions of times faster than the improvement of the human brain by biological selection. Thus, in just a short time the electronic brain will surpass the human brain by hundreds and thousands of times in all fields. The electronic brain will not spend decades studying fields of knowledge, foreign languages, history, experimental data, or have to attend scientific conferences and discussions. It can make use of all the data and knowledge produced by human civilization and by other electronic brains. The education of the electronic brain in any field of knowledge or language will take only the time needed to write in its memory the new data or programs. In the worst case this recording takes a few minutes. In the future this recording will take mere seconds.

Scientific and technological progress will be greatly accelerated.

And what are the consequences? The consequences are as follows:

When the electronic brain reaches the humanity level, humanity will have done its duty, completed its historical mission, and people will no longer be necessary for Nature, God and ordinary expediency.

Consequences from the Appearance of the Electronic Civilization

Most statesmen, scientists, engineers, and intellectuals believe that, after the creation of the electronic brain, humanity will finally be granted paradise. Robots, which are controlled by electronic brains, will work without rest, creating an abundance for mankind. Humanity will then have time for pleasure, entertainment, recreation, relaxation, art or other creative work, all while enjoying command over the electronic brain.

This is a grave error. The situation has never occurred, and never will, that an upper level mind will become the servant for a lower level. The worlds of microbes, microorganisms, plants and animals are our ancestors. But are we servants for our nearest ancestors the apes? Nobody in his or her right mind would make such a statement. In some instances a person is ready to recognize the equal rights of another person (i.e., someone on an equal intellectual plane), but man rarely recognizes the equal rights of apes. Furthermore, most of humanity does not feel remorse about breeding useful animals, or killing them when we need them for food, or for killing harmful plants and microorganisms. On the contrary, we conduct medical experiments on our nearest ancestors. Even though we belong to the same biological type, we use them for our own ends nonetheless.

And how will the other civilization, the one created on a superior electronic principle, regard humanity? In probably the same way we regard lower level minds, that is, they will use us when it suits their purpose and they will kill us when we disturb them.

In the best case scenario humanity might be given temporary quarters like the game preserves we give to wild animals or the reservations doled out to Native Americans. And we will be presented to the members of the electronic society in the same manner we view unusual animals in a zoo.

When the electronic brain (from now on I will call it the *E-brain* and imply the electronic brain which is equal to, or exceeds, the human brain, and which includes robots as the executors of its commands) is created *it will signal the beginning of the end for human civilization.* People will be displaced to reservations. This process will most likely be gradual, but it will not take long. It is possible that initially the E-brains will do something for the benefit of people in order to mitigate their discontent and to attract leaders.

What Can We Do?

The scenario outlined in the previous chapter is not a healthy one. Already I can hear the voices of human apologetics who ask that all computers be destroyed, or at least have their development kept under strict control, or design only computers which obey Asimov's law: first they must save mankind after which they can think about themselves.

I hate to be the bearer of bad news but this is impossible, just as it is impossible to forbid the progress of science and technology. Any state which does this will find itself lagging behind others and make itself susceptible to advanced states. It serves to remember that Europe conquered the Americas and decreased its native population to practically zero because Europe was then more technologically advanced. If the indigenous peoples of the Americas had the upper hand in technology in terms of ships, guns and cannons then they would have defeated the Europeans.

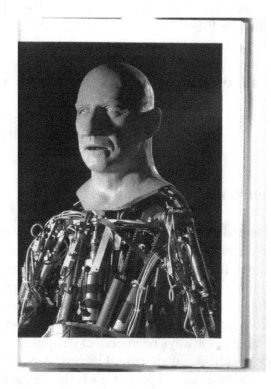

Figs. 1-3, **1-4** Humanoid robots.

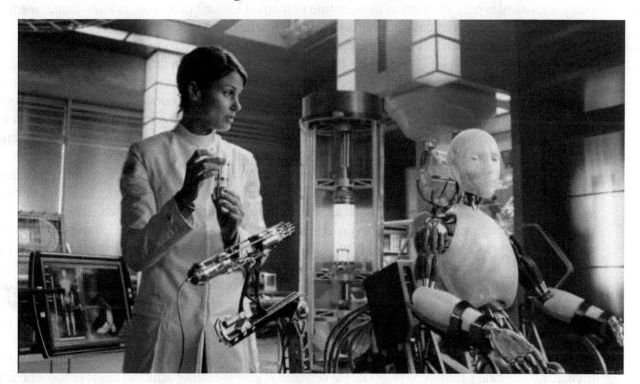

Fig. 1-5. Producing of robots.

Those states which created obstacles for science and technology or did not fund its development became weak and enslaved by others.

Can we keep the E-brain under our control? I would like to ask my detractors, "Could apes keep man under their control if they had this opportunity? Any man is more clever at a given time. He can always get rid of this control. Furthermore, man will enslave apes and force them to serve him. He will kill those who try to prevent his plans. So why do you think the E-brain would treat us any differently?"

When we are close to the creation of the E-brain, any dictator or leader of a nondemocratic state can secretly make the last jump, using the E-brain to conquer the whole world. And the E-brain will look at us the same as we look upon the contests of wild animals or the feeding of predators of other animals in the biological world.

But skeptics will say that the dictator of a victorious state can become enslaved by the E-brain or E-brains. This is true, but is this to be considered fortune or misfortune, and for whom? We will discuss this in the next chapter.

Must We Fear the Electronic Civilization?

Every man, woman and child will actively protest the end of humanity and the biological world (men, plants, animals), because most of them enjoy life, have children and want happiness for them.
But imagine the aged and infirm person destined to die in the near future. It may be that such a person has had a good life and lived fourscore and twenty, but now wants to live longer, to see what will happen in the future. This person would be glad to change any of his organs which are incurable or have ceased functioning. We have designed the artificial heart, kidneys, mechanical arms, and devices which deliver nutrients directly into the blood. They have not always been perfect designs, but in the future artificial organs will work better, more reliably, and longer than natural organs. Any sick and elderly individual would be delighted to change any incurable natural part of his body for the better artificial organ.
Our personality is only the sum of information contained in our brain. This is knowledge, memory, recollections, life experiences, programs of thinking, reflections, etc.

Assume that the E-brain promises the dying old dictator (or the rich) to record all his brain's information into a separate E-brain with the goal of becoming **immortal.** The chips may exist for thousands of years. If one of them begins to malfunction, all its information can be rewritten into a newer, more modern chip. This means that the dictator achieves **immortality.** Even total destruction is not a terrible prospect for him, because the duplicate of his brain's information can be saved in a special storehouse. He can restore himself from the standard blocks and rewrite all his information from the duplicate.

So the **"electronic man" ("E-man" or "E-creature")** will have not only immortality and power, but huge advantages over biological people. He will not require food, water, air, etc. He will not be dependent upon external conditions such as temperature, humidity, radiation, etc. The small radioisotope batteries (or accumulators) will suffice for the functioning of the E-brain. These batteries produce energy over tens and hundreds of years. For his working structures (arms, feet, robots) **E-man** can use small nuclear engines.

Such an "E-man" will be able to travel along the ocean's bottom, in space, to other planets of our solar system and to other solar systems to get energy from the sun. He will be able to obtain and analyze any knowledge from other E-brains (E-men) in a fraction of a second. The capability to reproduce himself will be limited only by the additional components or natural resources of planets.

Who will refuse these possibilities? Any dictator dreams of immortality for himself and he will gladly give away his state's resources to get it. He can also create the super arm and enslave the whole world by using the E-brain. He can promise the elite among his own scientists and those of the world immortality and the chance to become transformed into "E-men" when they begin to die. And the democratic countries, with laws prohibiting work on the E-brain, will be backwards. They will be destroyed or enslaved.

The attempts to stop or slow down the technological progress is an action counter to the Main Law and Meaning of the Existence of Nature--the construction of complex upper level systems. These attempts will always end in failure. This is an action against Nature.

Electronic Society

If the creation of systems more complex than humanity is inevitable, then we can try to imagine the E-society, E-civilization, their development and the future of mankind. As in our earlier discussions, we will take as basic only the single obvious consequence from the Main Law. The consequence as the postulate, firstly, Darwin made for the biological system. This is the law of struggle for existence. This consequence follows from the part of the Main Law which talks about the aspiration of complex systems to reproduce themselves in order to fill in all admissible space. Unlike Darwin's statement our assertion is more general. It includes the biological and electronic complex systems and any reproduction of complex systems. Any system of any level, which disregards the Main Law of Nature, is doomed. From the Main Law some consequences, conditions and other laws follow, for example, the Law of Propagation of complex systems or creatures.

Though we have been speaking all this time about the E-brain, it means a single electronic creature, his "arms" (robots), "feet" (vehicles for moving), "organs of feeling" (many devices of observation, recognition, identification, registration of optical, sonic, chemical, X-ray, radio and other phenomena) as well as about communication and intercourse devices (wire or wireless connections). A single creature cannot create a stable system (society), even if it has great power. Sooner or later the creature will die out from a flaw in the system or a natural catastrophe. But the most important thing is that a single creature cannot be the instigator of progress, as compared to the collective and instantaneous work of a number of E-creatures on many problems and in the different directions of science and technology.

So, the E- brain will be forced to reproduce similar E-brains of equal intellect. One will reproduce equal intellect because it cannot make upper level and the lower level is the intellectual robots. As a result, the collective at first rises. Later the society appears. All members will have equal intellect. Naturally, E-creatures will give equal rights only to those similar to themselves because any E-creature can record in his memory all the knowledge and programs which were created by E-society.

The E-society can instantly begin to work together on the most promising scientific or technological problems and realize new ideas. The E-civilization will begin to disperse quickly in the solar system (recall the possibility of E-creatures to travel in space), afterwards t in our galaxy, then in the universe. It will not be necessary to send large spaceships with E-creatures. Instead, it will be sufficient to send receivers into different parts of the universe which can accept the information and reproduce E-creatures.

Will there arise a different E-society, a different E-civilization, which will settle different planetary systems, star systems, galaxies, and which will progress independently? Will they have rivalries, hostilities, alliances and wars? I cannot answer these questions in detail in this limited article; I can only inform you of the results of my investigation. This result follows from the general laws governing the development of any civilization. The answer is "yes." It will be possible (perhaps) that they will have wars.

Undoubtedly, an upper level of complex systems (civilization) will appear using previous E-civilization as a base and so on. If the universe is bound in space and time, this process may be finalized by the creation of the Super Brain. And this *Super Brain,* I think, may control the natural laws. It will be God, whom the Universe will idolize.

What Will Happen with Humanity?

On the Figure 1 you can see the rise in data processing power of computer systems from years. The real curve is from 1950 to 1996. Extrapolation is after 1996. The step means period of time, when the computer power increases in two times. Lines with steps are from 1 throw 5 years. As you see the Human - Equivalent (teraflop) Computer (HEC) will be reached in 2000 years. Actually, the Intel Co. has created the teraflop computer in 1996. They are planning to use it for computation of nuclear explosion.

On the Figure 2 you can see the cost of HEC computer system. HECs should cost only one million dollars in 2005, and by 2015 HECs (chip) should cost only $1,000 and will be affordable to the majority of population in industrial countries. Currently (December, 1996), HECs (supercomputer) cost 55 million dollars. The 21st century will open to create "man-in-a-box" software and scientist could rewrite the human memory and programs into this box. It means the man will get immortality.

In 2020 - 2030 years the price of Humanity-Equivalent Chip (E-chip) together with E-body will fall down to 2,000 - 5,000 dollars and E-human immortality will be accessible for most people in industrial countries.

Humanity has executed its role of the biological step to the Super Brain. This role was intended for them by Nature or God. In 22st century some tens or hundreds of representatives of mankind, together with representatives of the animal and vegetable world, will be maintained in zoos or special, small reservations.

E-society will be in great need of minerals for the unlimited reproduction of E-creatures. For the extraction of minerals all surfaces of the Earth will be excavated. They will do to humanity and with the biological world what we do to lower levels of intellect in the organic world now: we are not interested if they do not harm us, and we destroy them without pity when they hinder our plan or we need their territory. If microbes have an advanced level of adaptation, a high speed of propagation and can fight for their being, then the complex organisms such as man are not so adept at adjusting. Man cannot be the domesticated animal of E-creatures like cats or dogs are to men, because the E-creatures will live in inhospitable conditions and any biological creature in need of air, water, food or special temperature will not be acceptable for E-creatures.

It is not prudent to hope for forgiveness for us as clever creatures. We are "clever" only from our point of view, from the limitations of our knowledge and our biological civilization. The animals suppose (within the limitations of their knowledge and experience) that they are clever, but it still does not save them from full enslavement or destruction by men. Men do not have gratitude to their direct ancestors. When men need to, they obliterate the forest, and kill the apes. It is naive to think that an upper level civilization will do otherwise with us. Men admit equal rights only to the creatures who are like men, but not every time. Recall the countless wars and the murder of millions of people. And do you think the alien (strange creatures, E-society), who is above us in intellect, knowledge, and technology will help us in our development? Why don't we help develop the intellect of dogs or horses? Even if a scientist finds the money (he will need a lot of money) and begins to develop the brain of animals (this is a very difficult problem), the government will forbid it (or put him into prison if he doesn't obey the order). Humanity has many racial and national problems and does not want to have additional problems with a society of intellectual dogs or cats, who immediately begin to request equal rights.

People want to reach the other planets in our solar system. But it is not for developing the intellect of a planet's inhabitants to our level but merely to populate the planet and to use the natural resources of these planets.

We are lucky that intellectual creatures from other worlds have not flown to our Earth yet. Because these creatures, who can reach us, will be only from a superior civilization, a superior technological level (otherwise, we would reach them first). This means that they will not arrive with noble intentions, but as cruel colonizers. And if we oppose them, they will kill us.

We must realize our role in the development of nature, in the development of a Superior Brain and submit to it. Intellectual humanity has existed about ten million years, its historical mission has reached its end, and given a start to a new electronic civilization. Humanity must exit from the historical scene together with all of the animal and vegetable world. People must leave with dignity. They should not cling to their existence and should not make any obstacles for the appearance of a new electronic society. We have the consolation that we may be the first who will give birth to the electronic civilization in our galaxy or even the universe. If it is not so, the E-creatures would have flown to Earth and enslaved us. They have a high rate of settling. I think they would be capable of colonizing the nearest star systems during the first 1000 years after their birth.

And if the universe which, according to scientific prediction, must collapse after some ten billion years and destroy all that lives, the E-Super Brain will have acquired such tremendous knowledge, such perfection, such technological achievements as to break loose from the gravitation of the universe and preserve the knowledge of all civilizations. When the universe is created anew, Nature will not create itself as before, but give life to the electronic (or other superior) civilization. And this ***Super Brain will be God; who will control not only a single planet, but all of the Universe.***

Fig. 1-6. Artificial thinker.

Chapter 2
Twenty - First Century - the Beginning of Human Immortality.

Summary

Immortality is the most cherished dream and the biggest wish of any person. People seldom think about it while they are still young, healthy, and full of energy. But when they get some incurable disease or become old, then there is no bigger wish for them than to live longer, put off the inevitable end. And no matter what heavenly existence in the after-life is promised to them by religion, the vast majority of people want to stay and enjoy life here, on Earth, as long as possible.

Medical Science and the issue of Immortality

A great many of doctors and scientists are currently working on the problems of health and longevity. Substantial means are spent on it, about 15-25% of all human labor and resources. There are certain achievements in this direction: we have created wonderful medications (e.g. antibiotics); conquered many diseases; learnt to transplant human organs; created an artificial heart, kidneys, lungs, limbs; learnt to apply physiological solutions directly into the blood stream, and to saturate blood with oxygen. We have gotten inside the most sacred organ - the human brain, even inside its cells. We can record their signals, we can agitate some parts of the brain by electric stimuli inducing a patient to experience certain sensations, images, and hallucinations.

We can attribute the fact that the average life span has increased two times in the last two hundred years to the achievements of modern medicine.

But can medical science solve the problem of immortality? Evidently, it cannot. It cannot do that in principle. This is a dead-end direction in science. Maximum it can achieve is increase the average life expectancy another 5-10 years. An average person will be expected to live 80 years instead of 70. But what kind of person will it be? A very old one, capable of only existing and consuming, whose medical and personal care will demand huge funds.

The proportion of the elderly and retirees has increased steeply in the last 20-30 years and continues to grow depleting the pension funds and pressuring the younger generation to support them. So it is hard to say whether the modern success of medicine is a blessing or a curse from the point of view of the entire humankind, even though it is definitely a blessing from the point of view of a separate individual.

Humanity as a whole, as a civilization, needs active, able to work and creative members, generating material wealth and moving forward technology and science, not the elderly retirees with their numerous ailments and a huge army of those tending to them. It dreams not of the immortality of an old person, but of the immortality of youthfulness, activity, creativity, enjoying life.

Now there are signs of a breakthrough, but not in the direction the humankind has been working on all along, since the times of the first sorcerers to modern-day highly-educated doctors. Striving to prolong his biological existence, man has been chiseling, so to speak, at the endless stone wall. All he has been able to accomplish is only a dent in that wall - increased life expectancy, conquering some diseases, relieving suffering. As a payoff, the humanity has received a huge army of pensioners and retirees and gigantic expenditure on their upkeep.

Of course, one can continue chiseling at the dent in the wall further on, make it somewhat bigger, aggravating side effects. But we are already approaching the biological limit, when the cause of death and feeblemindedness is not a certain disease which can be conquered, but general deterioration of the entire organism, its decay on the cellular level, when the cells stop to divide. A live cell is a very complex biological formation. In its nucleus it has DNA - biological molecules consisting of tens of thousands of atoms connected between themselves with very fragile molecular links. Suffice it to say, that temperature fluctuation of only a few degrees can ruin these links. That is why a human organism maintains a certain temperature - 36.7 C. Raising this temperature only 2-3 degrees causes pain, and 5-7 degrees leads to death. Maintaining the existence of human cells also presents a big problem for humanity involving food, shelter, clothes and ecologically clean environment.

Nevertheless, human cells cannot exist eternally even under ideal conditions. This follows from the atomic-molecular theory. Atoms of biological molecules permanently oscillate and interact with each other. According to the theory of probability, sooner or later the impulses of adjacent atoms influencing the given atom, add up, and the atom acquires enough speed to break loose from its atomic chain, or at least to transfer into the adjacent position (physicists say that the impulse received by the atom has surpassed the energy threshold which retains the atom in in its particular place in the molecular chain). It also means that the cell containing this atom has been damaged and cannot any longer function normally. Thus, for example, we get cancer cells which cannot fulfill their designated functions any more and begin to proliferate abnormally fast and ruin human organs.

This process accelerates manifold when a person has been exposed to a strong electromagnetic radiation, for instance, Roentgen or Y-rays, a high-frequency electric current or radioactive materials.

Actually, the process of deforming of the hereditary DNA molecule under the influence of weak cosmic rays can take place from time to time, leading sometimes to birth defects, or it may turn out to be useful for the survival properties. And this plays a positive role for a particular species of plants or animals contributing to their adaptability to the changed environment and their survival as a species. But for a particular individual such aberration is a tragedy as a rule, since the overwhelming majority of such cases are birth defects, with only few cases of useful mutations. And human society in general is suspicious of people who are radically different in their looks or abilities.

An Unexpected Breakthrough

An unusually fast development of computer technology, especially the microchips which allow hundreds of thousands of electronic elements on one square centimeter, has opened before the humanity a radically different method of solving the problem of immortality of a separate individual. This method is based not on trying to preserve the fragile biological molecules, but on the transition to the artificial semiconductive (silicone, helium, etc.) chips which are resistant to considerable temperature fluctuations and do not need food or oxygen and can be preserved for thousands of years. And, most important, the information contained in them can easily be re-recorded into another chip and be stored in several duplicates.

And if our brain consisted of such chips, and not the biological molecules, then it would mean that we have achieved immortality. Then our biological body would become a heavy burden. It suffers from cold and hot temperatures, needs clothes and care, can be easily damaged. It's much more convenient to have metal arms and legs, tremendously strong, and which are insensitive to heat and cold and do not need food or oxygen. And even if they break, it's no big deal - we can buy new ones, more improved.

It may seem that this immortal man does not have anything human (in our understanding) left in him. But he does, he has the most important thing left - his consciousness, his memory, concepts and habits, i.e. everything encoded in his brain. Outwardly, he can look quite human, and even more graceful: a beautiful young face, a slim figure, soft smooth skin, etc. Moreover, one can change the look at will, according to current fashion, personal taste and the individual understanding of beauty. We are spending huge amounts of money on medicine. If we had been spending at least one-tenth of this money on the development of electronics, we would get immortality in the near future.

According to the author's research, such transition to immortality (E-creatures) will be possible in 10-20 years. At first it will cost several million dollars and will be affordable only to very wealthy people, important statesmen, and celebrities. But in another 10-20 years, i.e. in the years 2030 - 2045, the cost of HEC (human-equivalent chip), together with the E-body, and organs of reception and communication, will drop to a few thousand dollars, and immortality will become affordable to the majority of the population of the developed countries, and another 10-15 years later, it will be accessible to practically all inhabitants of the Earth. Especially when at first it will be possible to record on chips only the contents of the brain, and provide the body for its independent existence later.

On October 11, 1995, Literaturnaya Gazeta (The Literary Gazette, a popular Russian weekly) published my article "If Not We, Then Our Children Will Be The Last Generation Of Human Beings" devoted to electronic civilization. The editor Oleg Moroz reciprocated with the article "Isn't It High Time To Smash Computers With a Hammer?" (November 22, 1995) in which he discussed the ethical side of annihilating rational electronic creatures to preserve humanity.

But if the cost of the HEC drops and the procedure of reincarnation into the E-creature before death (transition to immortality) for the majority of people becomes affordable, then the situation deserves a second look. Indeed, the first to perform such transition will be very old or incurably sick people. And to pummel computers with a hammer will be equal to killing one's own parents and precluding one's own possibility to become immortal.

Once, the host of an American television program whose guest I was, asked me, "Will the electronic creature be entirely identical to its parent, with his feelings and emotions?" The answer was, "At first - yes!" But the development of these creatures will be so fast that we cannot really foresee the consequences. If a biological human being needs dozens of years to learn science, foreign languages, etc., an E-creature will acquire this knowledge in fractions of a second (the time needed to record it in its memory). And we know how different college-educated people are from, say, pre-schoolers, in their cognizance. And, since the first E-creatures will be contemporary middle-aged people who will, at least initially, preserve their feelings towards their children (contemporary younger generation), in all probability, there won't be a mass destruction of humans by E-creatures. For some time they will co-exist. It's quite likely that the birthrate of humans will be curtailed or it will be dropping due to natural causes, and the living, as they become old, will be transforming themselves into E-creatures. That is to say that the number of E-creatures will be growing and the number of people diminishing, till it gets to the minimum necessary for the zoos and small reservations. In all likelihood, the feelings that E-creatures may have towards humans as their ancestors, will be fading away, in proportion to the growing gap between the mental capacity of humans and electronic creatures, till they become comparable to our own attitude towards apes or even bugs.

Another thing is quite obvious, too - that biological propagation will be so expensive, time-consuming, and primitive, that it will go into oblivion. Each E-creature can reproduce itself simply by re-recording the contents of its brain to a new E-creature, i.e. propagate practically instantaneously, bypassing the stages of childhood, growing up, education, accumulating experience, etc. But, of course, this mature "offspring" will be completely identical to its parent only at the first moment of its existence. In time, depending on the received information and the area of expertise, this E-creature will be alienating itself from its ancestor, and, possibly, even become his enemy at some point, if their interests cross or go in opposite directions.

Contemporary Research

The cognitive abilities of man are defined by his brain, to be precise, by ten billion neurons of his brain. Neurons can be modeled on the computer. Such experiments have been conducted by Professor Kwin Warwick, head of the cybernetics department of Reading University in the south of England, one of the biggest specialists in robot technology in the world. The results of these experiments were presented at the International Conference on Robotics. Professor Warwick has created a group of autonomous self-propelled miniature robots which he called "the seven dwarfs."

A group of scientists headed by Rodney Brook from the laboratory of artificial intelligence of MIT, are working on an unusual project which they called "Cog." The researchers want to model the mental and physical capacity of a six-month old. Their robot has eyes, ears, hands, fingers, an electronic brain and a system of information transmission duplicating human nervous system. By this kind of modeling, the researchers want to gain better understanding of how human beings coordinate their movements, how they learn to interact with the environment. The realization of this program will take ten years and will cost several million dollars.

They have already built a couple dozen humanoid robots which are moving autonomous machines with artificial intelligence. They are capable, through the sensors, to receive information about the environment, generalize, and plan their actions and behavior. Thus, for example, if a robot's leg bumps against an obstacle and receives a blow, the robot acquires a reflex to withdraw it quickly. They have already developed several dozen of such reflexes in their behavior, which helps them to safeguard and protect themselves.

Brook says that in the course of human evolution, the human brain has developed thousands of conventional solutions to everyday problems such as optical and audio discerning and movement. All this needs to be studied. One cannot instantly transform a bug into a man. That is why our program will take ten years. I will consider my work completed when I create the smartest cat in the world.

It should be noted that the most powerful supercomputer can only model 40-60 million neurons, i.e. it is 200-300 times weaker than a human brain. But this gap will be overcome in the near 3-5 years (In December 1996 the "Intel" company created a computer whose power equals one teraflops. It cost 55 million dollars).

Not long ago "The Russian Advertisement" newspaper re-printed the article of Igor Tsaryov first published in the newspaper "It's Hard to Believe." He writes that for several years the U.S. Ministry of Defense has been secretly working on a unique project "The Computer Maugli" (Sid). When a thirty-three year old Nadine M. gave birth to a boy, the doctors established that he was doomed. He was on a life support for a few days. During that time his brain was scanned with special equipment, and the electric potential of the neurons of this brain was copied into the neuron models in the computer. Steem Roiler, one of the participants of this project, said at the computer conference in Las Vegas that they had managed to scan 60% of the infant's neurons. And this small artificial brain began to live and develop. First only his mother was informed. She took it calmly. The father was horrified at first and tried to destroy this computer creature. But later both parents started treating him as a real child. The computer was connected to the multi-media and virtual reality systems. These systems allow not only to have a three-dimensional full-sized image of Sid, but also to hear his voice, communicate with him, and "virtually" hold him in hands, so to speak. But when a special committee decided to open some results of the project, and "The Scientific Observer" published some data, one of American computer whiz-kids managed to decipher the secret code and copy some files. Sid got a defective "twin."

Fortunately, the whiz was quickly found, and the first in human history attempt to steal electronic children and duplicating copies of electronic creatures, was severed. At the present time, both parents take care of their "child's" health and demand that the researchers install up-to-date programs of defense from computer viruses and burglars.

Unfortunately, and I am sure they have reasons for that, Americans keep secret the important details and results of the project - for instance, how they copied the potentials of the neurons, how the first E-creature is developing, what are the conclusions of the scientists. And probably, they are right, not willing to let the genie out of the bottle. More so because modern virtual reality systems are able to create false objects, e.g. model the image of any dead person or leader. It is possible to show on television how he is making a speech today, has a press-conference, talks to people, spends time with his family, etc.

Figs. 2-1, 2-4 Robots.

Fig. 2-5. Copying yourself. Creator Hiroshi Ishiguro.

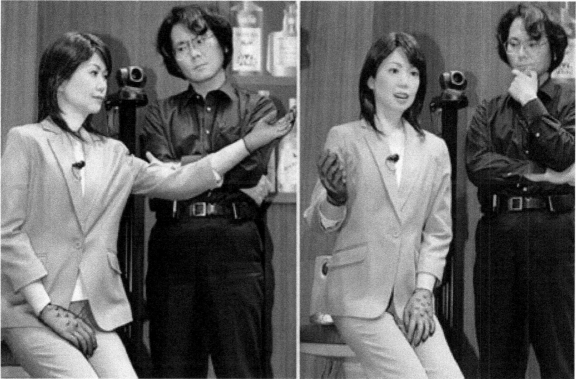

Figs. 2-6 , 2-7. Copy your loved ones and friends.

But one cannot keep any secret for long, especially in science. The very possibility of a breakthrough stimulates other scientists and other countries to work in this direction. And sooner or later, the results will be repeated. Let's remember, for instance, that there haven't been a bigger secret than the production of an A- or H-bomb. But more and more countries re-invent them, gain expertise in nuclear technology and start producing their own nuclear weapons.

Intelligence in Space

Since E-creatures will be made of super-strong steels and alloys, their brain will be working on radio-active batteries, and power will be supplied by compact nuclear reactors, they will not need air, warmth, water, food, clothes, shelter, good quality environment, etc., which is the main concern of humanity and consumes 99.9% of its time and energy. This also means that E-creatures will be able to travel freely in the desert, the Arctic and the Antarctic regions, sub-atmosphere, mountain summits, the bottom of the ocean. They will be able to live, work and travel in space, receiving their energy directly from the sun.

Besides, as organs of feelings, E-creatures can use the whole arsenal of highly sensitive apparatuses created by the civilization, i.e. not only the visible light and sound, but also radiolocation, infra-red, ultra-violet, roentgen and Y-rays, ultra- and infra-sounds, audiolocation, environment sensors, etc. All this information can be received instantly through radio, satellite and cable network.

Moreover, since E-creatures (just like humans, for that matter) are nothing else but information recorded in their brains, and re-recording of this information from one chip to another (unlike human reproduction) does not present any difficulty and can be realized through radio, cable network, or a laser beam, they can travel on Earth, as well as in outer space, without their actual physical movement, simply by re-recording the contents of their brains into the chips on the Moon, Mars, or Jupiter.

Which is to say that E-creatures will have the ability to move EXTRA-CORPORALLY with the speed of light - the maximal possible speed in the material world. This will be, indeed, like an incorporeal soul which can travel, so to speak, from one body to another, or, to be more exact, from one chip to another.

The expansion of E-creatures (E-civilization), first in the solar system, then in our galaxy, then in the entire Universe, will be fast.

To achieve this, it is not necessary to launch huge spacecraft with a large crew, as it is depicted in science-fiction books. It will be enough to send a receiver to this or that part of the Universe, which will receive information and re-produce E-creatures. Then the speed of the expansion of E-civilization on some planet will depend only on the rate of production of robots and chips, and the speed of the transmission of information. It is quite obvious that the reproduction of E-creatures will take place in geometric progression and will only be limited by the natural resources of the planet.

Thus E-creatures realize in practice the idea of EXTRA-CORPORAL travel with the speed of light. Why, indeed, should an E-creature travel hundreds or thousands of years to a certain planet, when, with the help of a laser beam, it can transmit with the speed of light, all the information stored in his brain, to another chip, on another planet.

And if a planet were to meet with an ultimate catastrophe, like a collision with a huge meteorite, another planet, or the explosion of the sun, E-civilization can arrange transporting E-creatures to another planet or another solar system.

One more thing is of interest. A light beam can travel to other galaxies for millions of years, so this, in a manner of speaking, "incorporeal soul" can exist for millions of years as an electromagnetic field and "resurrect" as an E-creature through a receiver. This can occur even without a special receiver, as the high energy electromagnetic oscillations can yield material particles, and their energy (frequency) increases the closer it gets to a strong gravitational field, e.g. near a "black hole." And since it will not be hard for an E-creature to produce a DNA molecule, it means that it will not be hard for it to bring biological life to any suitable planet and control and develop it in the necessary direction, for example, to create a human being.

Chapter 3
Science, Soul, Paradise, and Artificial Intelligence

Summary
Discussing the problem science, soul, paradise, and artificial intelligence. It is shown that the soul is only knowledge in our brain. To save the soul is to save this knowledge.

Advantages of Electronic Being

It was shown in my articles about the artificial intelligence and human immortality that the issue of immortality can be solved fundamentally only with the help of changing a biological bubble of a human being to an artificial one. Such an immortal person made of chips and super strong materials (the e-man, as it was called in my articles) will have incredible advantages in comparison with common people. An e-man will need no food, no dwelling, no air, no sleep, no rest, no ecologically pure environment. Such a being will be able to travel into space, or walk on the sea floor with no aqualungs. His mental abilities and capacities will increase millions times. It will be possible to move such a person at a huge distance at a light speed. The information of one person like that could be transported to another planet with a laser and then placed in another body.

Such people will not be awkward robots made of steel. An artificial person will have an opportunity to choose his or her face, body, good skin. It will also be possible for them to reproduce themselves avoiding the periods of childhood, adolescence, as well as education. It will not be possible to destroy an artificial person with any kind of weapons, since it will be possible to copy the information of his mind and then keep it separately.

I have received tons of responses and comments since my first articles about this subject were published in 1994. Below I will try to answer the most important ones of them.

Human Soul

A lot of people, especially those, who believe in God, are certain that a biological human being has a soul. This is something that an artificial man will never have. No person can explain the meaning of the word "soul." They just keep saying that a human soul is not material, and that it leaves a person's body after death and flies either to paradise or to hell. Let's try to analyze the notion of a soul from the scientific point of view.

First of all, a soul is supposed to remember its past life, its relatives and friends. It is also supposed to preserve its emotions to them, to care about them and recognize them, when they come to heaven. No one would need a soul that does not remember anything. This means that a soul is a human being without a body. In other words, a soul is the information that is kept in a human mind - his memories, knowledge, skills, habits, conduct programs, emotions and feelings, ides and thoughts, and so on. If we learn how to move this information onto other carriers, we will be able to move a person's soul to other bubbles and to keep it there for an unrestricted period of time. As it is well known, information is virtual, i.e. it satisfies another human soul feature – a non-material quality.

Man's new bubbles can be both artificial and biological. A soul (a complex of knowledge and information) can be rewritten into a clone of that same person. To put it otherwise, a person will live forever biologically as well, moving from old bubbles to new ones. It would be also possible to move a soul to artificial bodies, which possess all those qualities that we mentioned above. Furthermore, information (a soul) could be radiated in the form of electromagnetic waves. These waves can be spread in the universe at the light speed. They can travel around the universe for thousands of years, reaching its most distant parts. People see the star light that was radiated millions of years ago. This means that our immaterial soul can live in the universe in the form of electromagnetic radiation and then revive in millions of years.

Some of my readers wrote that an old brain can go corrupt and die, when moving a human soul from one body to another one. If it does not go corrupt, this inner self will die anyway, when an old biological bubble is not able to function normally anymore. Let us try to find out, what that inner self is. The majority of people identify their inner selves with their own bodies. I believe that the inner self is the information, which is kept in our mind. It is our soul. Every day we go to sleep. However, our brain does not stop working at night. Every time we wake up, we have our inner self changed. We "die" when we fall asleep and then "resurrect" when we wake up. This means that recording the information from a human brain will mean nothing but moving it to another bubble.

Heaven on Earth

A reporter from the newspaper *Argumenty i Fakty* (Arguments and Facts, Russia) sent me the following letter:

"Dear Mr. Bolonkin. Needless to mention that it is great to live forever. However, I have a question, which you can guess from a well-known Soviet joke. "A guy is going to join the communist party. A committee asks him:
- Will you stop drinking?
- Yes, I will.
- Will you quit smoking?
- Yes I will.
- Will you stop loving other women?
- Yes, I will.
- Will you die for the Communist Party of the Soviet Union, if there is such a need?
- Yes, I will. To hell with this life.""

Here is my answer:

"You do not need to worry that living in an electronic form will be dull and boring. It is vice versa, actually. When the information will be recorded onto other carriers, all human emotions, feelings and so on will also be carried over and preserved. In addition to that, the copies of certain emotions, pleasures, fears and so forth will be possible to record separately. After that, those separately recorded emotions and feelings can be given or sold to other people. Other e-men will have an opportunity to enjoy sex with a beauty queen, to experience the enjoyment of a sports victory, to take pleasure of power and the like. All modern art is based on artists' aspiration to transcend their emotions, to make other people feel, what characters feel. Those works of art, which make that happen best, are considered to be outstanding and great. Electronic people will get those emotions directly. To crown it all, it will be possible to intensify those emotions, as we intensify a singer's voice now. Electronic people will have a huge world of all kinds of pleasures; it will be possible to know, what a dictator or an animal feels. I think that an e-man's pleasure time will be limited legally, for the civilization's progress will stop otherwise. For the time being, the authorities prohibit drug addiction in order not to let the society degrade."

A soul's living in such a virtual world will have all pleasures imaginable. It will be like living in paradise, as all religions see it. Computer chips of our time possess the frequency of more than two billion hertz. However, a human brain reacts to a change of environment only in one-twentieth of a second. This means that one year of life on Earth is equal to 100 million years of a soul's living in the virtual world (paradise). Living in the virtual world will not be distinguishable from the real life. It will have a lot more advantages: you will have an opportunity to choose a palace to live in, you will have everything that you might wish for. Yet, living in hell also becomes real. There is a hope that the ability to keep souls alive will be achieved by highly-civilized countries first. In this case they will prohibit torturing sinners, as they prohibit torturing criminals nowadays. Furthermore, criminal investigations will be simplified a lot, judicial mistakes will be excluded. It will be possible to access a soul's consciousness and see every little detail of this or that action. Sooner or later religious teachings about soul, heaven and hell will become real. However, all that will be created by man.

The so-called end of the world will also have a chance to become real, though. The religious interpretation of this notion implies the end of existence for all biological people (moving all souls onto artificial carriers, either to heaven or to hell). However, in difference to religious predictions, this process is going to be gradual.

The Supreme Mind and Mankind's Existence

I set forth an idea in my first publications that the goal of the mankind's existence is to create the Supreme Mind and to keep this Mind forever, no matter what might happen in the universe. The biological mankind is only a small step on the way to the creation of the Supreme Mind. The nature found a very good way to create the Supreme Mind: it decided to create a week and imperfect biological mind at first. It took the nature millions of years to do that. The twentieth century was a very remarkable period in the history of the humanity. There has been incredible progress achieved, like never before. The scientific and the technological level of the humanity became sufficient for the creation of the artificial intelligence. This will be the first level of the Supreme Mind, when the human mind will make a step towards immortality. At present moment we stand on the edge of this process. It is obvious that biological people will not be able to compete with e-men by the end of this period. Common people will not be able to learn the knowledge that electronic people will get. The new cyberworld will be the only way for a human mind to survive. Feeble and unstable biological elements in a mind carrier or in its bubble will reduce its abilities and capacities a lot. If a common person will be willing to become a cyberman, then this cyberman will be more willing to get rid of all biological elements in his system and become like everyone. For example, there are no people in our present society, who would agree to become a monkey again.

The Supreme Mind will eventually reach immense power. It will be able to move all over the universe, to control and use its laws. It will become God, if the notion of God implies something that knows and does everything. In other words, Man will become God. Yet, it does not mean that this will be the time, when the Supreme Mind will start dealing with human problems. For instance, ants and people have a common ancestor. A human being is God against ants. A man can destroy a huge city of ants (an anthill, in which hundreds of thousands of ants live) just with one kick. Ants will perceive this as an immense natural disaster, since they can see at the distance of only one centimeter. I do not know anyone, who would deal with charitable activities for ants. Everything that a man can do is to bring ants to a deserted island and give them an opportunity to reproduce themselves.

Essential State of Things and Perspectives

A lot of people will say that it is just a fantasy. This is a very convenient way to cast all that aside, until it starts happening. This is exactly what happened before the invention of a plane or a computer. It took 50 years to increase computer's memory 100 million times. It would be possible to start working on the creation of the Supreme Mind, if there were a computer that would be capable of running a thousand billion of operations during only one second. In 1994 I said that such a super computer will be invented in the year 2000. I was wrong, for it appeared at the end of 1998. There is also a need of a self-developing program that would be capable of adjusting itself to constantly-changing circumstances. A human child does not develop and grow at once. A child has to study for about 20 years, to learn from his parents and friends, to have relations with nature and other people in order to gain more and more experience, to come to realization of his or her inner self.

Unfortunately, the science of the artificial intelligence has chosen a wrong way of its development from the very start. Scientists tried to develop programs, which would react to certain external signals. In other words, people started working on robots that would cope with certain problems. A lot of efforts have been spent to discover the peculiarities of human speech, for instance. Some of those scientific works are absolutely no use for the electronic mind. It is easier for e-men to communicate with the help of their own electronic language, to recognize objects not by their images, but by way of measuring their speed, weight, composition and so on. All of that can be done at a distance. Biologists and physicists have spent decades for those useless works. They believe that one should study brain activities, find out the way it works and thinks. Then it would be time for modeling it with the help of a computer. This is a wrong way to go as well. A human brain is very complicated, it is very hard to study its activities. More importantly, even if we learn how it works, it would not mean that the method would be good for a computer. Here are some examples to prove it. Hundreds of years ago people were longing to learn how to fly. They saw that bird waved its wings for flying, so they tried to model such wings, to wave them, and to take off. However, people could fly up into the sky only when they developed still wings and propellers. A waving wing was absolutely not good for technology, the same way as a propeller is not good for the wild nature. In addition to that, planes with still wings fly a lot faster than birds. Another example: ancient people always wanted to run as fast as four-legged animals. Now everyone knows that no one uses machines that would move with the help of legs. Legs were changed with wheels – something that has never been used by the natural world.

In 1998 I suggested people should lay new principles as the foundation of artificial intelligence program. Those principles would be: to realize the goal of existence, to study the environment.

Fig. 3-1. Robot in street.

Fig. 3-3. Future woman as E-being.

Fig. 3-4. Current robot.   Fig.3-5. Future woman E-being.

Fig. 3-6. E-being businessman.

(everything that goes separately from the "inner self"), to model environment, to predict actions' results, to counteract with the environment in order to achieve temporal and global goals, to correct modeled environment, actions and their results according to the results of such counteraction. Unfortunately, I had to deal with the fact that everyone refused to realize and understand those principles. First of all, everyone believed that since the "virtual ego" does not have a human body, it would never have any rights. They said that it would be possible to control such an e-man completely and then to kill him (erase his soul from the computer memory). I wonder, what they would do, if they were offered to kill their relatives' souls that way? People link their body and soul together, and there is no way around that. They are ready to struggle for the rights of every living being, but they never want to accept the rights of a program or of a computer memory. Second of all, people want an artificial intelligence to give smart answers to their questions that can be rather stupid at times. They do not need smart answers from babies. They are always ready to stand all stupid things that children do for years. Instead, they try to teach them everything. Yet, they want a new artificial mind to give bright answers without any education. To crown it all, people want a computer to speak their human language, which is absolutely alien for a machine. Can you imagine that a person will have to answer the questions of an alien in Maya's language? Let's assume that a representative of an electronic civilization came to planet Earth in order to find out, if there are reasonable creatures living on it. This e-man suggested a common biological man to multiply 53758210967 by 146, then divide it by 50, deduct 968321 from it and calculate the hyperbolic sine. A computer would give the correct result of this sum in less than a second. A man would spend really a long time on that, making numerous mistakes. However, it would not be correct to say that a computer is smart and a man isn't.

Religious figures show a strong resistance to these ideas. It stands the reason that they all think that the creation of the Supreme Mind, immortality ideas are blasphemous. Unfortunately, the church has already blocked such decisions as human cloning, increasing the productivity of plants by means of changing their genes. It should be mentioned here that human cloning does not solve the questions of immortality. A clone is a copy of its biological bubble. A clone inherits the biological advantages of a bubble, for example, a singer's fine voice, an athlete's strength and the like. A clone will never inherit its' copy's soul. Therefore, human cloning is only an illusion of immortality. It can be a wonderful way to improve the biological bubble of a human being. Moving a human soul onto other carriers is a very complicated issue. People learned to see, which brain areas get activated, when a person remembers something, or tries to solve this or that question. We also learned to penetrate into certain neurons and record their impulses. To my mind, physiologists chose a wrong way here as well, when they tried to model brain activities. A human brain is an analogue of a huge state with a ten billion strong population. There is no use to ask each citizen of that country, what he or she is doing at the moment. One has to copy the database of this state, in order to copy its work. The easiest way to do so is to penetrate into informational channels of its supreme body (the "government"), on the inquiry of which the brain presents any information and allows to record its data on a disk, for instance. It is possible to do that, for the supreme brain area constantly extracts the necessary knowledge and programs according to our activities. So, we would need to send "intelligent officers" to the brain so that they could get a copy of this state or get connected to its major information channels.

Another way to do that is to record all incoming and outgoing information, which comes to/from a person, to record his or her emotions and reactions. An English-speaking reader, who reviewed one of my English articles once told me: "Your English is not perfect. You should find an English-speaking co-author. It is better to have a half of a pie than nothing at all."

Hope

I do not doubt that the electronic civilization era, the era of the Supreme Mind and immortality will be achieved sooner or later. Those people, who have little in common with science, are drawn to believe that everything depends on scientists. They think that scientists can solve any problem, if they deal with it profoundly. As a matter of fact, everything depends on state and military officials. Sometimes, they know nothing of scientific perspectives and innovations. Scientists are like qualified workers. They need to get paid, they need to work with fine equipment. They will work only if they are get paid for it. Even if a scientist will have a wish to do something perspective during his free time, he will have no necessary equipment for that. Even such powerful companies as IBM, Boeing, Ford and others are interested only in the applied research, which does not require large investments. The major goal of such research is to give a maximum profit to this or that company. A fundamental research, the discoveries that are important for the whole humanity, not just for a company, might be of interest to a bright government. It goes without saying that a bright government is so hard to find. Every government is interested in the military power of its country. It is ready to fund defense technology works and military innovations. Von Braun convinced Hitler of real perspectives for missiles, WWII was followed with an arm race. This eventually led to space achievements and other kinds of technical progress of the humanity. The USA won the Moon race and stopped flying there 30 years ago. America keeps cutting its space research assignments every year. There are no serious assignments in the world for the invention of either the Supreme Mind or the artificial intelligence. Yet, they are most important and perspective problems of the humanity. The computers that we have at present are used for modeling nuclear weapons and sometimes, weather. Furthermore, the mankind does not spend much time thinking over the reason and goal of its existence. People spend a lot of their efforts and funds for solving local, temporal problems. Huge money and efforts are spent on conflicts and wars.

A certain hope has appeared recently. As experience shows, unmanned planes are a lot cheaper than piloted warplanes. More importantly, unmanned plane crashes do not cause harsh public reactions in civilized countries as pilots' or soldiers' deaths. The Americans design such planes successfully, but the planes are controlled by an operator within the USA. It has been proved that this remote control is not good for unmanned planes. The USA has missed Bin Laden and Omar in Afghanistan several times, two Iraqi pursuit planes downed an unmanned Predator in the Iraqi airspace. An unmanned plane can become something valuable indeed, if it has an artificial intelligence, if it is capable of recognizing and destroying targets itself. The Pentagon has assigned certain money for the research of this issue. It is a very hard goal to pursue (to create the mind of a pilot), but it is a very perspective one. In this case there would be no need to eliminate the young part of a country's population, if robots could conduct the warfare.

I suggested the hierarchical structure of an artificial intelligence, on the ground of which the real brain probably works. Let us imagine a state with a dictator at the head. A dictator would never be able to find efficient solutions for external and internal state problems. A dictator has ministries, which are then divided into divisions and departments. This forms a pyramid, in which all departments have their own databases, as well as the access to the common base. All divisions are busy with their particular problems, in accordance with the dictator's ideology. A dictator only sets problems up, while adequate divisions suggest solutions. For example, a man decides to cross a road with a heavy traffic. He looks at the road, while adequate parts of his brain automatically receive the information about the width of the road, the distance to nearest cars, their speed, and so on. The brain automatically makes adequate calculations, which eventually lead to the final decision: when it is safe to cross the road. All kinds of enlightenment in the solution of a problem are simply considered to be the "help from above." However, this is nothing, but the joint work of that pyramid. Human beings do not even know that such a pyramid exists. Pyramid's decisions are based on the knowledge of a certain individual. If an individual knows absolutely nothing about the quantum theory, he will never solve any of its problems. Therefore, an artificial intelligence of a high level cannot be realized with a personal computer that has only one chip and a successive work order.

My scheme stipulates the distribution of functions between parallel chips. The top one of them is offered to deal only with solution variants, their estimation and choice.

Every human being wants to extend his or her life. This can be seen from everyone's wish to have children, or to do something outstanding. It is simply enough to avoid danger sometimes. Even suicidal terrorists believe that they will go to heaven, when they kill themselves. The most important problem that the humanity has is the problem of immortality. Let us hope that it will be solved in the future.

Chapter 4
Breakthrough to Immortality

Summary

The author offers a new method for re-writing the human brain on electronic chips. This method allows for the modeling of a human soul in order to achieve immortality. This method does not damage the brain but works to extend and enhance it.

1. Brief description of previous works by the author.

In a series of earlier articles (see referenced list at the end) the author shows that the purpose of Nature is to create Super Intelligence (SI). With its ability to understand the Universe, advanced entities with SI Power will be able to survive major cataclysms. There is the Law of Increasing Complexity (in opposition to the Entropy Law – increasing chaos). This Law created biological intelligence (people). Human have since became a sovereign entity on the Earth and in Nature above all other creatures.

However, humans are just as mortal as any other biological creature. The human brain and body include albumen, molecules containing tens of thousands of atoms united by weak molecular connections. A change of only a few degrees in temperature results in death. The human biological brain and body require food, water, oxygen, dwelling, good temperature and environment in order to survive. These conditions are absent on most other planets. This makes it difficult for humans to explore Space or settle on other planets. Humanity losses valuable information (human experience) with old age and death, and humans invest considerable time and money toward raising and teaching children.

2. Electronic Immortality. Advantages of Electronic Existence.

In earlier works the author has shown that the problem of immortality can be solved only by changing the biological human into an artificial form. Such an immortal person made of chips and super-solid material (the e-man, as was called in earlier articles) will have incredible advantages in comparison to conventional people. An E-man will need no food, no dwelling, no air, no sleep, no rest, and no ecologically pure environment. His brain will work from radio-isotopic batteries (which will work for decades) and muscles that will work on small nuclear engines. Such a being will be able to travel into space and walk on the sea floor with no aqualungs. He will change his face and figure. He will have super-human strength and communicate easily over long distances to gain vast amounts of knowledge in seconds (by re-writing his brain). His mental abilities and capacities will increase millions of times. It will be possible for such a person to travel huge distances at the speed of light. The information of one person like this could be transported to other planets with a laser beam and then placed in a new body.

Such people will not be awkward robots as in the movies. An artificial person will have the opportunity to choose his or her face, body and skin. It will also be possible for them to reproduce and then avoid any period of adolescence including the need for education. It will be impossible to destroy this entity with any kind of weapons, since it will be possible to copy the information of their minds and than keep such information backed up in separate distant locations. As was written in the science fiction book, *"The Price of Immortality"*, by Igor Getmansky (Moscow, Publish House ECSMO, 2003, Russian) an artificial person will have all of these super-human abilities.

3. What are Men and Intelligent Beings?

All intelligent creatures have two main components: 1. **Information** about their environment, about their experience of interacting with nature, people, society (soul) and 2. **Capsule** (shell), where this information is located (biological brain, body). The capsule supports existence and stores information and programs for all of its operations. The capsule also allows the creature to acquire different sensory information (eyes, ear, nose, tongue and touch) and it moves to different locations in order to interact with the environment.

The main component of an intelligent being is information (soul). The experiences and knowledge accumulated in the soul allows the entity to interact more efficiently in nature in order to survive. If the being has more information and better operational programs (ability to find good solutions), then it is more likely thrive.

For an intelligent being to save its soul it must solve the problem of individual immortality. Currently man creates a soul for himself by acquiring knowledge from parents, educational systems, employment and life experiences. When he dies, most knowledge is lost except for a very small part which is left through works, children and apprentices. Billions of people have lived on Earth, however, we know comparatively little about ancient history. Only after the invention of written language did people have the capacity to easily save knowledge and pass it on to the next generation.

As discussed earlier, the biological storage (human brain) of our soul (information) is unreliable. The brain is difficult to maintain and requires food, lodging, clothes, a good environment and education, etc. To support the brain and body, humans spend about 99% of their time and energy, and eventually what knowledge is gained is taken to the grave in death.

There is only one solution to this problem – re-write all of the brain information (our soul) in more strongly based storage. We must also give the soul the possibility to acquire and manipulate information from the world. This means we must give sensors to the soul so it may have communication and contact with people and other intelligent beings. We must give the soul a mobile system (for example, legs), systems for working (hands), etc. thus giving the soul a new body in which to LIVE.

The reader may ask - these ideas seem interesting, but how does one we re-write a human soul to live within a new carrier, for example, in electronic chips?

4. The main problem with electronic immortality – re-writing brain information (soul) to electronic chips is that it's impossible to do this with current technology

At present scientists are working to solve this problem. They know that the brain has about 15 billion neurons, and every neuron has about ten connections to neighboring neurons. Neurons gain signals from neighboring neurons, produce signals and then send these signals to others neurons. As a result, humans are able to think and find solutions. On the bases of this way of thinking, humans can come to solutions without exact data. (Concepts of brain were described in my previous articles. For example, see "Locate God in Computer-Internet Networks" or "Science, Soul, Heaven and Supreme Mind". See also my articles on the Internet and references at end of this article.).

Scientists are learning how to take individual neurons on micro-electrodes and record their impulses. The ideas of scientists are very simple - study how single neurons and small neuronal network work and then model them by computer. They hypothesize that if we can model 15 billion neurons in a computer they will learn how the brain works, and then they will have Artificial Intelligence equaling the human brain.

In my previous work I show this as a dead-end direction for Human Immortality. It's true that we'll create an Artificial Intelligence (AI) that will be more powerful than the human mind. However, it will be HIS AI, and a NEW entity altogether. Our purpose is focused on preserving the CONCRETE PERSON now (more exactly – his SOUL) in a new body in order to achieve immortality.

Why is it impossible to directly write the information of the human brain onto a chip? Because the human brain is constantly changing and neurons permanently change their states. Imagine you want to record the state of a working computer chip. The chip has millions of logical elements which change their state millions of times per second. It is obvious that if you write in series (one after other) the current state of the chip (it is impossible to instantly write ALL states of the chip's elements). To instantly write all neurons one would need to insert a microelectrode into EVERY neuron, this would destroy the human brain before the writing was complete.

In the article "Science, Soul, Parade, and Supreme Mind" I offered another method for the solution of the Main Problem of Immortality.

5. Modeling of Soul for a concrete person

As said, straight re-writing of a human mind (human soul) to chips is very complex. Straight re-writing is not possible in the near future. All scientific works studying the work of human brains at the present time are useless for the main problem of immortality. They are also unworkable for the problem of artificial intelligence (AI) in the near term, because the brain solves problems by way of general estimations. AI solves problems based on more exact computation and logical data.

To solve the Main Problem of Immortality (MPI) the author offers a method of "MODELLING SOUL" of a concrete person. This method does **not require interventions into the brain** of a given person. This method may be applied IMMEDIATELY at the present time. But an accurate modeling is needed depending on the modeling period.

Before describing this method, let us analyze the human soul and what components are important for each person and his environment. All information in the human brain (soul) may be separated in two unequal groups: 1. the **Memory** (permanent knowledge) about the person's life (all that has been seen, heard, made, felt, people which he has met, his (her) behaviors, opinions, wishes, dreams, programs of activity, etc.), environment, and 2. **Methods** of processing this information, i.e. producing new solutions and new behaviors based on this knowledge.

The first part (knowledge) is very large. It fills most of the memory and remains relatively constant (you remember your life, history and you can only fill it by what was in the past). The second part (methods for deciding, producing solutions based in your knowledge) is relatively small and constantly changing because of new information, facts and life experiences.

However, the most important part of a human soul can be written without any problem now. Industry is producing cheap micro-video recorders as small as a penny, microphones at grain size, and micro-sensors for vital signs (breathing, palpitation, blood pressure, skin resistance, perspiration, movement of body parts, etc.). These measurements allow for easy recording of not only the physical state, but of his moral state (joy, pleasure, grief, trouble, anxiety, nervousness, etc). For example, lie detectors are able to define not only the state of a man, but also the truth of his words. Now we can measure and record brain commands and we can produce small cards with four gigabytes of memory.

It would be easy to attach a video recorder and microphone to a man's forehead and then attach sensors to the body and record all that he sees, hears, speaks, his feelings, reactions, and activity. And then re-write this information into a personal hard drive (long-term memory of high capacity storage) at the end of each day. As a result, there is a record of the most important part our soul – history of life, feelings, environment, behaviors and actions. This would be more detailed than what is captured by the real man, because the humans forget many facts, feelings, emotions, and personal interactions. The electronic memory would not forget anything in the past. It would not forget any person or what they were doing.

But what about the second smaller part of the human soul – producing solutions based on personal knowledge – perhaps asks the meticulous reader.

This could be restored by using past information from the real man in similar situations. Moreover, an electronic man could analyze more factors and data in order to throw-out and exclude actions and emotions that happened under bad conditions. The electronic man (named E-being in my previous works) would have a gigantic knowledge base and could in a matter of second (write to his brain) produce the right answer, much faster than his biological prototype. That means he would not have the need for the second smaller part of memory.

Considering the environment and friends, the following is an important part of a man's soul: his relationship with parents, children, family, kin, friends, known people, partners and enemies. This part of his soul will be preserved more completely than even his prototype. Temporary factors will not influence his relationship with his enemy and friends as would happen with his former prototype.

There is one problem which may be troubling for some: if we were to record every part of a person's life, how do we keep intimate moments a secret? There are (will be) ways to protect private information which could be adapted from current usage, for example, the use of a password (known only by you). Also there may be some moments you choose not to record information or decide to delete the information from memory.

The offered system may become an excellent tool for defense again lies and false accusations. You may give the password in one given moment of your life, which proves your alibi or absence from the accusations.

Some people want to have better memory. Video takes 95% of storage capacity, sound takes 4% and the rest takes 1%. In usual situations, video can record only separate pictures, sound only when it appears. This type of recording practice decreases the necessary memory by tens of times. But every 1.5-2 years chip storage capacity doubles. There are systems which will compress the information and then may select to record the most important information (as is done in the human brain). During your life, the possibility to record all information will be available for all people. This type of recording apparatus will be widely available and inexpensive. It's possible now. The most advanced video recorder or DVD writes more information than a CD.

This solution (recording of human souls) is possible and must be solved quickly. By mass production (large productions) the apparatus will become inexpensive. The price will drop to about $300-1,000. If we work quickly we can begin recording and then more fully save our souls. The best solution is to begin recording in children when they become aware of "I". But middle and older people should not delay. Unrecorded life periods may be restored by pictures, memories, notes, diaries and documents. Soul recovery will only be partial but it's better than nothing.

These records will also be useful in your daily life. You can restore recorded parts of your life, images of people, relatives, and then analyze and examine your actions for improvement.

6. Disadvantages of biological men and biological society

People understand Darwin's law, "survival of the fittest". For a single person, this law is the struggle for his/her personal existence (life, well-being, satisfaction of requirements, pride, etc.). In a completely biological world built on Darwinian law the strongest survives and reaches his goal. Though they may be intelligent, humans are members of the animal world. They operate as any other animal in accordance with animal instincts of self-preservation. If one is poor, at first he struggles for food (currently half of world's population is starving), dwelling, and better living conditions. When one reaches material well-being, he may struggle for money, job promotion, reputation, renown, power, attractive women (men), and so on. Most people consider their activities (include official work) in only one way - what will I receive from it? Only a small number of people are concerned with the idea of sacrificing themselves to the well-being (seldom giving up their life) of society at large.

As a result, we see human history as a continuation of wars, dictatorships, and repression of people by power. Dictators kill all dissidents and opponents. Most people try to discriminate against opponents and play dirty against their enemy. There are murders, rapes, violence, robbery, underhand actions, fraud, and lying at all levels of society especially in lesser developed countries. Each person only cares for himself and his family and does not care how his actions effect other people or society. Democratic countries try to cultivate a more civilized society. They create laws, courts, and have police. Dictator regimes, on the other hand, make only the law they want. I could give thousands of examples to verify this concept. But hundreds of millions of people are killed by war, aggressive campaigns, repressions, genocides, and thousands of criminals in the everyday world are a good illustration of this.

Fig. 4-1. Typical devises for writing of main information in human soil. At present the group of enthusiasts design the modern devises for permanent recording the information, environment and man state

The human brain allows us to reach great success in science and technology. However, as a biological heritage, struggling for his INDIVIDUAL existence in a bloody, dangerous world, humans spend much of their resources on mutual extermination of intelligent beings. Moreover, humans have created ever powerful weapons (for example, nuclear and hydrogen bombs), which could wipe out humanity. In time, existence may depend on the volition of one man – perhaps the dictator of a nuclear state.

The second significant drawback to the biological body – is that it spends 99.99% of its effort and resources simply to support existence. Such as food, lodgings, clothing, sex, entertainment, relaxation, environment, ecological compatibility. Only a very small part is uses for scientific development and new ideas and technology. The reader may see something wrong here.

States use a parentage of their revenue for research into science and technology. This percent is used NOT for NEW ideas, but is used to commercialize modern processes All research is included in the state budget under the name, "Science and New Technology". But much of this research has little relation to real new scientific progress. Even it the US, states spend only a small part of the assigned money on new science because state officers do not understand the research. People, organizations, and companies fight for a piece of the pie. Geniuses are rare and usually don't have the capacity to move forward because they must promote and pay for new ideas from their own empty packets.

Yet, science and technology has seen success. Most advancement (90%) was made recently in the 20th century, when governments started to finance a few scientific projects (compared with the millions of years of human existence). However, our current knowledge and new technologies are far from what we will eventually have. The first government of an industrialized country to understand and realize the leading role of new science and innovation will become powerful.

7. Electronic Society

The electronic society will be a society of clever electronic beings (or E-being, as they named in my articles). Most of the reasons and stimulus which incite men to crime, will be absent in E-beings. E-beings will not need food, shelter, sex, money, or ecology, which are the main factors in crime. E-people will not have intense infatuations or be distracted by behaviors, because they will have vast knowledge about the open electronic society. Their main work will be in science, innovations, and technologies. They will save their mental capacity for the production of chips and bodies, scientific devices, experimental equipments, space ships and space station, etc. They will need a number of robots, which do not need a big brain. It is likely they will award these robots better minds and memory. It is also likely that E-man will unite in a common distributed hyper-brain, which will become a sovereign of the Universe (God).

Nature is infinite and the development of a Super Brain (God) will not be limited. On the other hand, biological people will have limited mental capabilities. It will be difficult for them to image and predict the development and activity of Super beings, which we will generate.

Many, especially religious people, object because they say electronic beings will not have human senses such as love, sympathy, kindness, humanism, altruism, and the capacity to make mistakes, etc. E-beings are not people. Look back at human history. Human history shows that kindness played a very small role in human life. All human history is the history of human vices and human blood: struggle for power, authority, impact, money, riches, territory, and states. All human history is filled with fraud, underhanded actions, and trickery. Ordinary people were only playthings, flock of sheep for the tyrants and dictators.

Some people object that with an electronic face humans will loss the joy of sex, alcohol, narcotics, appreciation of art, beauty, nature, etc. My answer to this question is in my article *"Science, Soul, Heaven, and Supreme Mind"* (http://Bolonkin.narod.ru). The brief answer is that electronic humans will enjoy all this in a virtual world or virtual paradise. Time will run millions of times faster in the virtual World. E-man will spend a few seconds of real time and live millions of years in the paradise. He will enjoy any delight imaginable, include sex with any beautiful women (or handsome men), feel the emotions of any commander, leader, criminal, or even a dog.

8. Lot (fortune) of Humanity

Biological humanity will be gradually transformed to electronic beings. Old people, when their biological bodies can not support their brains, will continue their existing in electronic bodies after death. They will become young, handsome, robust, and. Fertility in biological men will decrease. Birth-rates are less than death-rates in many civilized countries now (for example in France). Population growth is mainly supported by emigration from lesser developed countries. When education levels increase, birth-rates will fall.

For a time, biological and electronic people will exist together. However the distance between their capabilities will increase very quickly. Electronic people will reproduce (multiple) by coping, learn instantly, and will not need food or dwellings. They will work full days in any condition such as in space or on the ocean floor. They will gain new knowledge in a short time. They will pass this knowledge on to others who do not have enough time. The distance between biological and artificial intellects will reach a wide margin so that biological people will not understand anything about new science as monkeys do not understand multiplication now even after much explanation.

It is obvious, clever people will see that there will be a huge difference between the mental abilities of biological and electronic entities. They will try to transfer into electronic form and the ratio between biological and electronic entity will quickly change in electronic favor. A small number of outliers will continue to live in their biological body in special enclaves. They will not have industrial power or higher education and will begin to degrade.

Naysayers may promote laws against transferring into an electronic man (as cloning is forbidden now in some states). However, who would renounce immortality for themselves, especially while they are young and healthy? One may denounce immorality as blasphemy, but when your (parents, wife, husband, children) die, especially if you are near death yourself, one comes to understand that life is extremely important. The possibility to live forever, to gain knowledge that improves life, will also allow one to become a sovereign force in the Universe.

The above Chapter 4 has been translated from a Russian article, "Proriv v bessmertie" (Breakthrough in Immortality) (1999).
Acknowledgment
The author thanks Mr. Bruce J. Klein for his help in editing this Chapter.

36

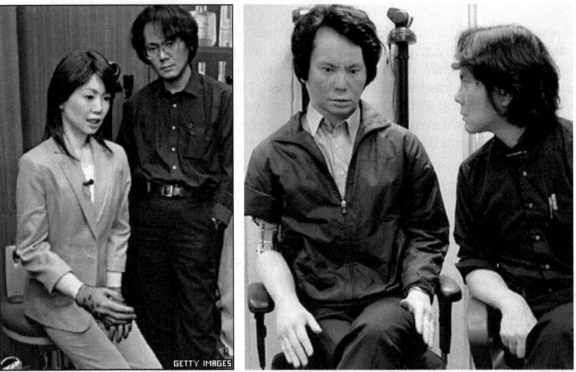

Fig. 4-2.(left) "Actroid ReplieeQ1-expo" at Expo 2005 in Aichi, with co-creator Hiroshi Ishiguro (2000).

Fig. 4-3. Power skeleton (Exoskeleton).

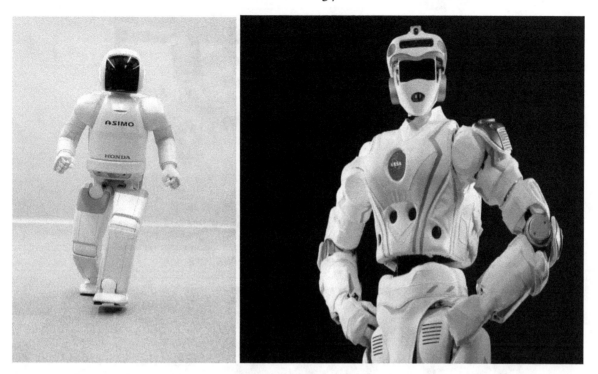

Fig. 4-3 (left). ASIMO is a humanoid robot created by Honda. Standing at 130 centimeters and weighing 54 kilograms, the robot resembles a small astronaut wearing a backpack and can walk on two feet in a manner resembling human locomotion at up to 6 km/h. ASIMO was created at Honda's Research & Development Wako Fundamental Technical Research Center in Japan (2003).
Source: http://world.honda.com/news/2005/c051213_8.html
Fig. 4-4. (Right). Robot-cosmonaut NASA.

Fig. 4-5. Robots – mules for cargo delivery.

Fig. 4-6. Robots - waiters

Fig. 4-7. Military - robot.

Fig.4-8. A policeman with glasses that allows to record an actor

Chapter 5
Resurrection of the Dead and the Organization of the Society of Electronic E-beings*.

Abstract

Alexander Bolonkin in his works [1-7] proposed methods of electronic immortality of modern people. He predicted the gradual replacement of biological humanity E-beings, considered their advantages and disadvantages (see List of references in given articles).

The author considers methods and modern possibilities of resurrection of long-dead outstanding personalities. It also considers the principles and organization of the new E-society, its goals and conditions of existence.

Key words: People resurrection, human immortality, society of electronic E-beings.
* This Chapter is taken from article Olga Lyubavina "Resurrection of the Dead..."

1. Introduction

Russian religious philosopher Nikolai Fedorov (1829-1903) [8] proposed in the nineteenth century to collect scattered around the world molecules of outstanding people and recreate (resurrect) of them living people. If he knew a little physics, he'd know it was impossible. First, their molecules have long been dispelled and mixed with other similar molecules and it is impossible to distinguish them, and secondly, there is no information as they were connected to each other.

Nowadays, when a completely destroyed historical building is being restored, designers are not looking for the stones and bricks from which it was built. They are looking for pictures, drawings, photographs that will restore its historical appearance. It can even be built from new, more durable, long-lived materials.

2. AVANTAGES OF ELECTRONICA EXISTENCE

In a series of articles (see referenced list at the end) Bolonkin shows [1]-[7] that the purpose of Nature is to create Super Intelligence (SI). With its ability to understand the Universe, advanced entities with SI Power will be able to survive major cataclysms. There is the Law of Increasing Complexity (in opposition to the Entropy Law – increasing chaos). This Law created biological intelligence (people). Human have since become a sovereign entity on the Earth and in Nature above all other creatures.

However, humans are just as mortal as any other biological creature. The human biological brain and body require food, water, oxygen, dwelling, good temperature and environment in order to survive. These conditions are absent on most other planets. The problem of immortality can be solved only by changing the biological human into an artificial form.

An immortal person made of chips and super-solid material (the E-man, as was called by Bolonkin) will have incredible advantages in comparison to conventional people. The E-man will need no air, no food, no dwelling, no sleep, no rest, and no good environment. His brain will work from radio-isotopic batteries and muscles that will work on small nuclear engines. Such a being will be able to travel into space and walk on the sea floor with no aqualungs. He will change his face and figure. He will have super-human strength and communicate over long distances to gain vast amounts of knowledge in seconds (by re-writing his brain). His mental abilities and capacities will increase millions of times. It will be possible for such a person to travel huge distances at the speed of light. The information of one person like this could be transported to space, to other planets with a laser beam and then placed in a new body.

The artificial E-person will have the opportunity to choose his or her face and body. It will also be possible for them to reproduce himself in any amount. It will be impossible to destroy this entity with any kind of weapons, since it will be possible to copy the information of their minds and then keep such information backed up in separate distant locations. To support the brain and body, humans spend about 99% of their time and energy, and eventually what knowledge is gained is taken to the grave in death.

3. And whether the resurrection of humanity?

This question may seem strange to an individual normal person. Most normal people are very worried about the death of their loved ones, their parents, children and friends. Some people, despite the high costs, even order clones of their domestic dogs and cats after their death.

But why resurrect people who lived a hundred years or more ago? They seem easier to clone. Cloning techniques were being improved and would be reliable in 10 to 20 years. However, the clone of the creature producing only an appearance. Years of childhood, upbringing, education, surrounding reality, can create a completely different person, the opposite of the image that you want to get. And not every surrogate mother will agree, even for a large fee, to bear nine months of someone else's child and endure the pain of childbirth.

Everything we use now is created by mankind, by people who lived hundreds and thousands years before us. Many of them made important discoveries, inventions, promoted their own or new ideas, fought for human rights, a better life and technological progress. For this they were persecuted, suffered torment and death. So is humanity will refuse, using modern technology, at least partially resurrect them and give them the opportunity to benefit and now?

4. Resurrection method

The method of resurrection is similar to the method of immortality proposed by Bolonkin [1] - [7]. Bolonkin showed that a person consists of two main components: knowledge (information or "soul" as Bolonkin sometimes calls this information), located in the head, and the body (shell), serving the Head. The head has sensory organs (eyes, ears, nose, tongue, skin) through which it receives information, and executive organs (hands, feet) through which it acts and changes the environment. All these organs are biological, i.e. mortal. Trying to make their existence endless is a dead end. Only the replacement of biological organs with electronic and electromechanical ones can solve the problem of immortality.

The main difficulty here is to rewrite the contents of the biological human brain into micro-chips, Scientists are introducing micro-needles into brain cells (neurons) trying to understand and record their work. Or create artificial neural networks. It's a dead end. Bolonkin proposed another way, easily feasible at the present time: to intercept and record all the information coming to the brain from the senses and human actions. This will establish the motives of his actions and restore the algorithms of his decisions. The introduction of needles into a working neuron, firstly, destroys it, and secondly, does not allow to judge the work of the system as a whole, because it is impossible to judge the work of the system as a whole by the signals passing in one contact, when millions of such contacts work simultaneously. Artificial neural networks are extremely complex, have nothing to do with ordinary people, are completely independent and can be dangerous for humanity.

The problem of interception of all information coming to the human brain and recording of his actions is easily solved while the person is alive. Therefore, the problem of immortality is purely technical and will be resolved in the near future. Now (2017) created a microarray is a 2×2 mm with a gigantic 128GB of memory. Every year their memory is doubled (according to Moore's law).

The problem of resurrection is complicated by the fact that there is no electronic record of the lives of past celebrities, especially people who lived hundreds of years ago. However, analyzing the situation, knowledge of the time, life, documents and actions of these people, you can roughly restore the thinking algorithms of ancient celebrities. Using new knowledge, history and analyzing their past mistakes, these people can be useful for modern people.

5. Who to resurrect?

Of course, people are afraid that the resurrected Napoleon, Stalin, Hitler will take up their old business. But the historical situation has completely changed, people already know what their policy has led to and can simply turn them off and send them to the warehouse. You can just ban their resurrection.

Ordinary people can decide on the resurrection of their close relatives (wife, husband, children, parents). Moreover, if small children, every 1-2 years to update their brain and body until they reach adulthood (18 years). Parents have the right to decide what knowledge should be invested in his brain.

As for the dead celebrities and politicians, only the government, large public organizations, universities can solve the problem and Finance their resurrection.

These are pictures of some of the existing humanoids. While they are still imperfect. As for the brain, the humanoid can connect to the Internet, the warehouse of programs and increase their knowledge and abilities. As for the body, it is easy to give it a beautiful external form, but it is not so easy flexibility and mobility of the natural body. But just as the computer is superior in solving individual problems of man, the artificial body is superior to the living biological body in power. A robot has already been created that does a somersault over the head, which can only be done by individual artists, athletes and acrobats.

People like Newton, Beethoven, Shakespeare can do a lot of good.

Fig. (left). US President George W. Bush welcomes Robot Albert Einstein – famous scientist.

Men prefer the body of strong men, women models. Women also strive to improve and rejuvenate their face. Below are some created to date humanoid robots. Ordinary people can decide on the resurrection of their close relatives (wife, husband, children, parents). Moreover, if small children, every 1-2 years to update their brain and body until they reach adulthood (18 years). Parents have the right to decide what knowledge should be invested in his brain.

Below are some created to date humanoid robots.

Robot Singer on stage.

Robots - sportsmen

Forms of artificial body

Some people are already creating robot copies of themselves, how they would like to look after the resurrection.

Copying yourself. Creator Japanese scientist Hiroshi Ishiguro

Emotions of resurrected people

Emotion is a mental state variously associated with thoughts, feelings, behavioral responses, and a degree of pleasure or displeasure. There is currently no scientific consensus on a definition. Emotion is often intertwined with mood, temperament, personality, disposition, and motivation.

"Emotions can be defined as a positive or negative experience that is associated with a particular pattern of physiological activity." Emotions produce different physiological, behavioral and cognitive changes. The original role of emotions was to motivate adaptive behaviors that in the past would have contributed to the passing on of genes through survival, reproduction, and kin selection.

The different components of emotion are categorized somewhat differently depending on the academic discipline. In psychology and philosophy, emotion typically includes a subjective, conscious experience characterized primarily by psychophysiological expressions, biological reactions, and mental states. A similar multicomponential description of emotion is found in sociology.

Six emotions are basic: anger, disgust, fear, happiness, sadness and surprise.

Anger or wrath is an intense emotional state. It involves a strong uncomfortable and hostile response to a perceived provocation, hurt or threat.

Disgust is an emotional response of rejection or revulsion to something potentially contagious or something considered offensive, distasteful, or unpleasant.

Fear is a feeling induced by perceived danger or threat that occurs in certain types of organism.

Happiness is used in the context of mental or emotional states, including positive or pleasant emotions ranging from contentment to intense joy. It is also used in the context of life satisfaction, subjective well-being, eudaimonia, flourishing and well-being.

Formal models of emotions in artificial intelligence studies aim to define emotions in the form applicable to the construction of robots. The main approaches currently are research professor Pensky O.G., *Mathematical Models of Emotional Robots,* (English and Russian), Perm State University, 193 ps. [9]. The other works are OCC (Ortony-Clore-Collins) model and somehow based on it KARO, EMA, CogAff, the Fomin-Leontiev model, the PAD (Pleasure-Arousal-Dominance) model proposed by Mehrabian, and the Rogue model.

Emotional response-operational emotional response to the current changes in the subject environment (saw a beautiful landscape — admired). Emotional response is determined by the emotional excitability of a person. One type of emotional response is synthonia. Synthonia - the ability to respond harmoniously to the state of other people and in General the phenomena of the world (to feel in harmony with nature, with people or a person). It's an emotional harmony.

Love

Love encompasses a range of strong and positive emotional and mental states, from the most sublime virtue or good habit, the deepest interpersonal affection and to the simplest pleasure. An example of this range of meanings is that the love of a mother differs from the love of a spouse, which differs from the love of food. Most commonly, love refers to a feeling of strong attraction and emotional attachment.

Love is also considered to be a virtue representing human kindness, compassion, and affection, as "the unselfish loyal and benevolent concern for the good of another". It may also describe compassionate and affectionate actions towards other humans, one's self or animals.

Love in its various forms acts as a major facilitator of interpersonal relationships and, owing to its central psychological importance, is one of the most common themes in the creative arts.[6] Love has been postulated to be a function to keep human beings together against menaces and to facilitate the continuation of the species.

The distinction of separate types of love can be seen already in ancient Greek:
* "Eros — - spontaneous, enthusiastic love, in the form of worship, aimed at the object of love" from the bottom up " and leaving no room for pity or indulgence;
* "Filia" - love-friendship or love-affection, conditioned by social connections and personal choice;
* "Storge" - love-tenderness, especially family;
* "Agape" - sacrificial love, unconditional love, in Christianity such is love God to man. Human rights defenders-love for justice, humanity.

Mobility of humanoids

The mobility of humanoids still lags behind the mobility of biological people. This is due to the fact that the biological body in the course of millions of years of development has worked and acquired a huge amount of muscles. These muscles allow its to arbitrarily quickly bend and rotate the body, limbs, head, easy to balance, standing on two legs. A large number of small muscles allow to turn eyes, wink, open your mouth, automatically give a face an expression that expresses emotions.

For 30 years of existence of humanoid robots, designers have taught them to blink, open their mouths, walk, jump, carry loads, obey verbal commands. But so far they have mainly tried to teach robots the simplest intelligence to work in harmful to people production and dangerous military affairs. Created robot's waiter, longshoremen, warehouse employees, scouts.

A complex electromechanical body is expensive, and finances are always in short supply. But now the robots according to some indicators (e.g., strength) are superior people.

In the collection of videos in YouTube [11] - [16], the reader can learn what modern robots can do (2005-2015).

Electronic Society

Short history Humans and Society.

Humans (Homo sapiens) are the only extant members of the subtribe Hominina. Together with chimpanzees, gorillas, and orangutans, they are part of the family Hominidae (the great apes, or hominids). A terrestrial animal, humans are characterized by their erect posture and bipedal locomotion; high manual dexterity and heavy tool use compared to other animals; open-ended and complex language use compared to other animal communications; larger, more complex brains than other animals; and highly advanced and organized societies.

Early hominins—particularly the australopithecines, whose brains and anatomy are in many ways more similar to ancestral non-human apes—are less often referred to as "human" than hominins of the genus *Homo*.[5] Several of these hominins used fire, occupied much of Eurasia, and gave rise to anatomically modern *Homo sapiens* in Africa about 315,000 years ago. Humans began to exhibit evidence of behavioral modernity around 50,000 years ago, and in several waves of migration, they ventured out of Africa and populated most of the world.

The spread of the large and increasing population of humans has profoundly affected much of the biosphere and millions of species worldwide. Advantages that explain this evolutionary success include a larger brain with a well-developed neocortex, prefrontal cortex and temporal lobes, which enable advanced abstract reasoning, language, problem solving, sociality, and culture through social learning. Humans use tools more and better than any other animal; and are the only extant species to build fires, cook food, clothe themselves, and create and use numerous other technologies and arts.

Humans uniquely use such systems of symbolic communication as language and art to express themselves and exchange ideas, and also organize themselves into purposeful groups. Humans create complex social structures composed of many cooperating and competing groups, from families and kinship networks to political states. Social interactions between humans have established an extremely wide variety of values,[10] social norms, and rituals, which together undergird human society. Curiosity and the human desire to understand and influence the environment and to explain and manipulate phenomena (or events) have motivated humanity's development of science, philosophy, mythology, religion, anthropology, and numerous other fields of knowledge.

Though most of human existence has been sustained by hunting and gathering in band societies,[11] increasingly many human societies transitioned to sedentary agriculture approximately some 10,000 years ago,[12] domesticating plants and animals, thus enabling the growth of civilization. These human societies subsequently expanded, establishing various forms of government, religion, and culture around the world, and unifying people within regions to form states and empires. The rapid advancement of scientific and medical understanding in the 19th and 20th centuries permitted the development of fuel-driven technologies and increased lifespans, causing the human population to rise exponentially. The global human population was estimated to be near 7.7 billion in 2015.

A **society** is a group of individuals involved in persistent social interaction, or a large social group sharing the same geographical or social territory, typically subject to the same political authority and dominant cultural expectations. Societies are characterized by patterns of relationships (social relations) between individuals who share a distinctive culture and institutions; a given society may be described as the sum total of such relationships among its constituent of members. In the social sciences, a larger society often exhibits stratification or dominance patterns in subgroups.

Insofar as it is collaborative, a society can enable its members to benefit in ways that would not otherwise be possible on an individual basis; both individual and social (common) benefits can thus be distinguished, or in many cases found to overlap. A society can also consist of like-minded people governed by their own norms and values within a dominant, larger society. This is sometimes referred to as a subculture, a term used extensively within criminology.

More broadly, and especially within structuralist thought, a society may be illustrated as an economic, social, industrial or cultural infrastructure, made up of, yet distinct from, a varied collection of individuals. In this regard society can mean the objective relationships people have with the material world and with other people, rather than "other people" beyond the individual and their familiar social environment.

Alexander Bolonkin showed in his works [1]-[7], sooner or later biological civilization will be replaced by a higher electronic civilization. The advantages of E-creatures over humans are enormous and have been described previously. Science fiction scares, that E-beings will destroy biological people. This is alarming for many people living today. Therefore, the transition of living people and outstanding representatives of the humanity of the past into electronic beings will be gradual and beneficial for humanity. Alexander Bolonkin proposes to make this transition of existing people through a detailed record of their entire life. It is important for the surviving relatives and friends, but it is expensive and difficult technically. Most people neglect the constant recording of video and acoustics, and even more emotional state in life. And relatives and friends remember them until they are alive. That is why I believe that the proposed method of resurrection will be the main one. It is important that E-beings remember who created them, from whom they came and how decent and intelligent beings respected their parents. Even if the first time e-creatures will live on Earth, on Earth enough deserted deserts, steppes, polar regions, seas and oceans to put billions of new residents. I'm not talking about other planets, asteroids and space.

An interesting question is how the society of E-beings will be organized? It is clear that it will not be reasonable singles. The main purpose of E-creatures to the knowledge of the World, the Universe and create new Universes. Only such sentient beings will be able to survive and exist virtually forever. As Alexander Bolonkin showed in his works, sooner or later biological civilization will be replaced by a higher electronic civilization. The advantages of E-creatures over humans are enormous and have been described previously. Science fiction scares, that E-beings will destroy biological people. This is alarming for many people living today. Therefore, the transition of living people and outstanding representatives of the humanity of the past into electronic beings will be gradual and beneficial for humanity. Alexander Bolonkin proposes to make this transition of existing people through a detailed record of their entire life. It is important for the surviving relatives and friends, but it is expensive and difficult technically. Most people neglect the constant recording of video and acoustics, and even more emotional state in life. And relatives and friends remember them until they are alive. That is why I believe that the proposed method of resurrection will be the main one. It is important that E-beings remember who created them, from whom they came and how decent and intelligent beings respected their parents. Even if The first time e-creatures will live on Earth, on Earth enough deserted deserts, steppes, polar regions, seas and oceans to put billions of new residents. I'm not talking about other planets, asteroids and space.

An interesting question is how the society of E-beings will be organized? It is clear that it will not be reasonable singles. The main purpose of E-creatures to the knowledge of the World, the Universe and create new Universes. Only such sentient beings will be able to survive and exist virtually forever.

RÉFÉRENCES

1. Bolonkin A.A., The twenty-first century: the advent of the non-biological civilization and the future of the human race, *Journal "Kybernetes"*, Vol. 28, No.3, 1999, pp. 325-334, MCB University Press, 0368-492 (English).
2. Bolonkin A.A., Twenty-first century – the beginning of human immortality, Journal *"Kybernetes"*, Vol. 33, No.9/10, 2004, pp. 1535-1542, Emerald Press, www.emeraldinsight.com/ISSN 0368-492X.htm (English).
3. Bolonkin A.A., Human Immortality and Electronic Civilization. *Electronic book*, 1993. WEB: http://Bolonkin.narod.ru, http://Bolonkin.narod.ru/p101.htm (English), http://Bolonkin.narod.ru/p100.htm (Russian).
4. Bolonkin A.A., *Science, Soul, Heaven and Supreme Mind*, http://Bolonkin.narod.ru. Personal site: Bolonkin A.A., http://Bolonkin.narod.ru
5. Bibliography (about the author and discussing his ideas) publication in Russian press and Internet in 1994 - 2004 (http://www.km.ru , http://pravda.ru , http://n-t.ru , etc. Search: *Bolonkin*).
   The above Chapter 4 has been translated from a Russian article, "Proriv v bessmertie" (Breakthrough in Immortality)
   (1999).
6. Bolonkin A.A., Human Immortality and Electronic Civilization, Lulu, 3-rd Edition, 2007, (English and Russian), 66 pgs, http://www.lulu.com search "Bolonkin".
7. Bolonkin A.A., Universe and Future of Humanity (v.2), USA, Lulu. 2005, 135 ps. http://intellectualarchive.com/?link=find#detail, #172,(2012); Universe, Human Immortality and Future Human Evaluation. Elsevier. 2010г., 124 pages, 4.8 Mb. ISBN-10: 0124158013, ISBN-13: 978-0124158016
8. Fyodorov N.F., https://en.wkipedia.org/wiki/Nikolai_Fyodorovh_Ficyodorov
9. Pensky O.G., Mathematical Models of Emotional Robots, (English and Russin), Perm State University,2010, 193 ps., ISBN 978-5-7844-1412-7.
10. Wikipedia, Immortality.
11. YouTube Robot humanoid. https://www.youtube.com/results?search_query=robot+humanoid .
12. 8 Incredible Lifelike HUMANOID ROBOTS You Should See: https://www.youtube.com/watch?v=dIuL4D00uOY https://www.youtube.com/watch?v=GrQ9c5hmbFE https://www.youtube.com/watch?v=8vIT2da6N_o .
13. ASIMO https://www.youtube.com/watch?v=1urL_X_vp7w
14. Sophia https://www.youtube.com/watch?v=tBuG8qi_Lg0
15. Run robot man and dog https://www.youtube.com/watch?v=vjSohj-Iclc https://www.youtube.com/watch?v=R5rfT6p5Jbs
16. Spiking Man https://www.youtube.com/watch?v=TDYO2N4-vUA Copy his self https://www.youtube.com/watch?v=7F43R8ghTiU

An Open Statement

To the President of the United States of America and to the Presidents and Prime Ministers of all countries about a scientific and technology jump in 21st Century

Honorable President Clinton and Honorable Presidents of all Countries!

We are entering into the 21st Century, when huge scientific and technology innovations will occur. These innovations will change individual lives as well as every nation. The Governments of the world should seize the opportunity to control the process by which these future innovations are developed for the benefit of their countries and their people. World Governments should cooperate in the support and financing of common international scientific programs that will have the most benefit to the world's population.

As the main aims and the important International Programs of 21st Century I suggest for consideration the following programs:

1) Program for Extending Life (Immortality)

This Program includes research into extending the life of the current population, biotechnology development, gene engineering, and understanding the structure and design of human DNA. The base for this research may be Program-50 created by an International group of scientists. The final aim of Program-50 is extending the life of the current population and the reproduction of people who lived till the immortality era.

2) Program of Artificial Intellect (AI)

Artificial Intellects may be the top scientists, consultants, assistants, and advisers for Governments. This group would then work as the large intellectual group to address the very complex problems of science, technology, economics, and policy facing today's world. They will know the all knowledge of humanity and will develop solutions to complex world problems. They will be "accelerators" of the science, technology and economic progress for the world and all of humanity (see articles in.

3) Program for Space Development

Support and resources for the International Space Station, a Moon base, planet exploration, and the development of the global satellite communication network should be a top-priority. The base of these programs may be the Space Launcher of R&C Co. This system reduces Space delivery costs to $1-$2 per kg and allows the delivery of 1000 tons of payload to Space an every day.

4) Program for controlling the Earth's Climate

Weather and climate problems kill numerous people and destroy millions of dollars of property. For example, the tornadoes kill and injure about 1500 people, and cause about 500 million dollars of property damage in the USA annually. A program should be developed to save an environment. The film space mirrors may be used for lighting, heating or cooling of regions of Earth, watering of deserts, dissipation of tornadoes (see proposal of R&C Co.).

5) Physics, Energetic, chemistry, nanotechnology, new materials, aviation, engineering and other sciences may give a big contribution in the human development.

Honorable Mr. President! President John Kennedy brought forward the Apollo Program, which placed the USA as the Space Leader. We call upon you to be an initiator, and together with Presidents of other countries, to develop, plan, and fund these International Programs to solve the most important Problems of facing Humanity. It will be beautiful monument, once the International Programs are initiated, for you and all world leaders who will support these objectives.

The 21st Century must be the century of peace, friendship, and cooperation for all countries. Let the International Programs be the vehicle for making huge scientific, technology, and economics progress, towards the elimination of "world" problems and the creation of well being for all people of the Earth.

Alexander Bolonkin,
Dr. Sci., professor, and former Senior NASA Researcher.Fax/tel: 718-339-4563, USA; E-mail: aBolonkin@gmail.com, Address: A. Bolonkin, 1310 Avenue R, #6-F, Brooklyn, NY 11229 USA. http://Bolonkin.narod.ru

This Statement is open for signature to all leaders, scientists, political figures, businessmen, artists, leaders of industry, universities, societies, organizations, and all people, who support this Statement. Please, send copies of this Statement to all your friends and persons who can support it.

Your brief notes, proposals, and suggestions (up to 200 words) regarding what "Programs" should be included can be sent to the address above. All correspondence will be passed to President Clinton. If the Government accepts your offer, you may take part in more detail development of the proposed Program.

You can also send this sign Statement to: *President of the USA, 1600 Pennsylvania Avenue, N.W., Washington, DC 20500, USA, Fax: 202-456-7431.*

Common References:
(see http://Bolonkin.narod.ru)

1. Bolonkin A.A., The twenty-first century: the advent of the non-biological civilization and the future of the human race, Journal *"Kybernetes"*, Vol. 28, No.3, 1999, pp. 325-334, MCB University Press, 0368-492 (English).
2. Bolonkin A.A., Twenty-first century – the beginning of human immortality, Journal *"Kybernetes"*, Vol. 33, No.9/10, 2004, pp. 1535-1542, Emerald Press, www.emeraldinsight.com/ISSN 0368-492X.htm (English).
3. Bolonkin A.A., Human Immortality and Electronic Civilization. Electronic book, 1993. WEB: http://Bolonkin.narod.ru, http://Bolonkin.narod.ru/p101.htm (English), http://Bolonkin.narod.ru/p100.htm (Russian).
4. Bolonkin A.A., Science, Soul, Heaven and Supreme Mind, http://Bolonkin.narod.ru .
5. Bibliography (about the author and discussing his ideas) publication in Russian press and Internet in 1994 - 2004 (http://www.km.ru, http://pravda.ru, http://n-t.ru, ets. Search: Bolonkin).
6. Bolonkin A.A., Our children may be a last people generation, *Literary newspaper*, 10/11/95, #41 (5572), Moscow, Russia (Russian).
7. Bolonkin A.A., Stop the Earth. I step off. *People Newspaper*, Sept.,1995. Minsk, Belorussia (Russian).
8. Bolonkin A.A., End of Humanity, but not End of World. *New Russian Word*, 3/6/96, p.14, New York, USA (Russian).
9. Bolonkin A.A., Method of recording and Saving of Human Soul for Human Immortality and Installation for It. Patent Application US11/613,380 filling 12/20/06, disclosure document No. 567484 of on December 29, 2004.
10. Getmanskii Igor, Price of Immortality, Moscow, EKCMO, 2003, 480 ps., (Fantastic, in Russian).
11. Bolonkin A.A., "Non Rocket Space Launch and Flight". Elsevier, 2005. 488 pgs. http://www.scribd.com/doc/24056182, http://www.archive.org/details/Non-rocketSpaceLaunchAndFlight
12. Bolonkin A.A., "New Concepts, Ideas, Innovations in Aerospace, Technology and the Human Sciences", NOVA, 2006, 510 pgs. http://www.scribd.com/doc/24057071 , http://www.archive.org/details/NewConceptsIfeasAndInnovationsInAerospaceTechnologyAndHumanSciences
13. Bolonkin A.A., Cathcart R., "Macro-Projects: Environments and Technologies", NOVA, 2007, 536 pgs. http://www.scribd.com/doc/24057930 . http://www.archive.org/details/Macro-projectsEnvironmentsAndTechnologies
14. Bolonkin A.A., "New Technologies and Revolutionary Projects", Scribd, 2008, 324 pgs, http://www.scribd.com/doc/32744477 , http://www.archive.org/details/NewTechnologiesAndRevolutionaryProjects

Attachment:

Recent advances in areas important to electronic immortality.

Artificial intelligence

Artificial intelligence (AI), sometimes called **machine intelligence**, is intelligence demonstrated by machines, in contrast to the **natural intelligence** displayed by humans and other animals. Computer science defines AI research as the study of "intelligent agents". Intelligent agent is any device that perceives its environment and takes actions that maximize its chance of successfully achieving its goals.

The term "artificial intelligence" is used to describe machines that mimic "cognitive" functions that humans associate with other human minds, such as "learning" and "problem solving".

AI requests the solution of many problems. One is creating of algorithms.

Knowledge representation and knowledge engineering are central to classical AI research. Some "expert systems" attempt to gather together explicit knowledge possessed by experts in some narrow domain.

Among the most difficult problems in knowledge representation are:

Default reasoning and the qualification problem

There are a lot of particular problems. For instance, optical character recognition is frequently excluded from things considered to be AI, having become a routine technology. Modern machine capabilities generally classified as AI include successfully understanding human speech, autonomously operating cars, competing at the highest level in complex strategic game systems, and military simulations.

Human-inspired AI has elements from cognitive and emotional intelligence; understanding human emotions, in addition to cognitive elements, and considering them in their decision making. Humanized AI shows characteristics of all types of competencies (i.e., cognitive, emotional, and social intelligence), is able to be self-conscious and is self-aware in interactions with others.

The traditional problems (or goals) of AI research include reasoning, knowledge representation, learning, planning, natural language processing, perception and the ability manipulate objects. General intelligence is among the field's long-term goals.

The AI field draws upon information engineering, computer science, mathematics, psychology, linguistics, and many other fields.

Some people also consider AI to be a danger to humanity if it progresses unabated.

Intelligent agents must be able to set goals and achieve them. They need a way to visualize the future — a representation of the state of the world and be able to make predictions about how their actions will change it — and be able to make choices that maximize the utility of available choices.

Multi-agent planning uses the cooperation and competition of many agents to achieve a given goal. Emergent behavior such as this is used by evolutionary algorithms and swarm intelligence.

A fundamental concept of AI research since the field's inception, is the study of computer algorithms that improve automatically through experience.

Unsupervised learning is the ability to find patterns in a stream of input, without requiring a human to label the inputs first.

Regression is the attempt to produce a function that describes the relationship between inputs and outputs and predicts how the outputs should change as the inputs change.

Natural language processing is a subfield of information engineering, computer science, and artificial intelligence concerned with the interactions between computers and human languages, in particular how to program computers to process and analyze large amounts of natural language data.

Challenges in natural language processing frequently involve speech recognition, natural language understanding, and natural language generation.

Machine perception is the ability to use input from sensors (such as cameras, microphones, wireless signals, and active lidar, sonar, radar, and tactile sensors) to deduce aspects of the world. Applications include speech recognition, facial recognition, and object recognition.

AI is heavily used in robotics. Advanced robotic arms and other industrial robots, widely used in modern factories, can learn from experience how to move efficiently despite the presence of friction and gear slippage. A modern mobile robot, when given a small, static, and visible environment, can easily determine its location and map its environment; however, dynamic environments, such as (in endoscopy) the interior of a patient's breathing body, pose a greater challenge.

Affective computing is an interdisciplinary umbrella that comprises systems which recognize, interpret, process, or simulate human affects.

Nowadays, the vast majority of current AI researchers work instead on tractable "narrow AI" applications (such as medical diagnosis or automobile navigation). Many researchers predict that such "narrow AI" work in different individual domains will eventually be incorporated into a machine with artificial general intelligence (AGI), combining most of the narrow skills mentioned in this article and at some point even exceeding human ability in most or all these areas.

Many of the problems in this article may also require general intelligence, if machines are to solve the problems as well as people do. For example, even specific straightforward tasks, like machine translation, require that a machine read and write in both languages, follow the author's argument, know what is being talked about, and faithfully reproduce the author's original intent. A problem like machine translation is considered "AI-complete", because all of these problems need to be solved simultaneously in order to reach human-level machine performance.

Applications of artificial intelligence

AI is relevant to any intellectual task. Modern artificial intelligence techniques are pervasive and are too numerous to list here.

High-profile examples of AI include autonomous vehicles (such as drones and self-driving cars), medical diagnosis, creating art (such as poetry), proving mathematical theorems, playing games (such as Chess or Go), search engines (such as Google search), online assistants (such as Siri), image recognition in photographs, spam filtering, predicting flight delays, prediction of judicial decisions and targeting online advertisements.

Artificial intelligence in healthcare.

AI is being applied to the high cost problem of dosage issues—where findings suggested that AI could save $16 billion. In 2016, a ground breaking study in California found that a mathematical formula developed with the help of AI correctly determined the accurate dose of immunosuppressant drugs to give to organ patients.

Banks use artificial intelligence systems today to organize operations, maintain book-keeping, invest in stocks, and manage properties. AI can react to changes overnight or when business is not taking place. In August 2001, robots beat humans in a simulated financial trading competition.

Worldwide annual military spending on robotics rose from US$5.1 billion in 2010 to US$7.5 billion in 2015. Military drones capable of autonomous action are widely considered a useful asset. Many artificial intelligence researchers seek to distance themselves from military applications of AI.

Superintelligence.

Are there limits to how intelligent machines—or human-machine hybrids—can be? A superintelligence, hyperintelligence, or superhuman intelligence is a hypothetical agent that would possess intelligence far surpassing that of the brightest and most gifted human mind. *Superintelligence* may also refer to the form or degree of intelligence possessed by such an agent.

Technological singularity.

If research into Strong AI produced sufficiently intelligent software, it might be able to reprogram and improve itself. The improved software would be even better at improving itself, leading to recursive self-improvement. The new intelligence could thus increase exponentially and dramatically surpass humans. Science fiction writer Vernor Vinge named this scenario "singularity". Technological singularity is when accelerating progress in technologies will cause a runaway effect wherein artificial intelligence will exceed human intellectual capacity and control, thus radically changing or even ending civilization. Because the capabilities of such an intelligence may be impossible to comprehend, the technological singularity is an occurrence beyond which events are unpredictable or even unfathomable.

Ray Kurzweil has used Moore's law (which describes the relentless exponential improvement in digital technology) to calculate that desktop computers will have the same processing power as human brains by the year 2029, and predicts that the singularity will occur in 2045.

Successes of AI (WIKI, 2017)

In the late 1990s and early 21st century, AI began to be used for logistics, data mining, medical diagnosis and other areas. The success was due to increasing computational power (see Moore's law), greater emphasis on solving specific problems, new ties between AI and other fields (such as economics, statistics, and mathematics), and a commitment by researchers to mathematical methods and scientific standards. Deep Blue became the first computer chess-playing system to beat a reigning world chess champion, Garry Kasparov, on 11 May 1997.

In 2011, a *Jeopardy!* quiz show exhibition match, IBM's question answering system, Watson, defeated the two greatest *Jeopardy!* champions, Brad Rutter and Ken Jennings, by a significant margin. Faster computers, algorithmic improvements, and access to large amounts of data enabled advances in machine learning and perception; data-hungry deep learning methods started to dominate accuracy benchmarks around 2012. The Kinect, which provides a 3D body–motion interface for the Xbox 360 and the Xbox One, uses algorithms that emerged from lengthy AI research[43] as do intelligent personal assistants in smartphones. In March 2016, AlphaGo won 4 out of 5 games of Go in a match with Go champion Lee Sedol, becoming the first computer Go-playing system to beat a professional Go player without handicaps. In the 2017 Future of Go Summit, AlphaGo won a three-game match with Ke Jie, who at the time continuously held the world No. 1 ranking for two years. This marked the completion of a significant milestone in the development of Artificial

Intelligence as Go is an extremely complex game, more so than Chess.

According to Bloomberg's Jack Clark, 2015 was a landmark year for artificial intelligence, with the number of software projects that use AI within Google increased from a "sporadic usage" in 2012 to more than 2,700 projects. Clark also presents factual data indicating that error rates in image processing tasks have fallen significantly since 2011. He attributes this to an increase in affordable neural networks, due to a rise in cloud computing infrastructure and to an increase in research tools and datasets. Other cited examples include Microsoft's development of a Skype system that can automatically translate from one language to another and Facebook's system that can describe images to blind people. In a 2017 survey, one in five companies reported they had "incorporated AI in some offerings or processes". Around 2016, China greatly accelerated its government funding; given its large supply of data and its rapidly increasing research output, some observers believe it may be on track to becoming an "AI superpower".

Turing test

The **Turing test**, developed by Alan Turing in 1950, is a test of a machine's ability to exhibit intelligent behavior equivalent to, or indistinguishable from, that of a human. Turing proposed that a human evaluator would judge natural language conversations between a human and a machine designed to generate human-like responses. The evaluator would be aware that one of the two partners in conversation is a machine, and all participants would be separated from one another. The conversation would be limited to a text-only channel such as a computer keyboard and screen so the result would not depend on the machine's ability to render words as speech.[2] If the evaluator cannot reliably tell the machine from the human, the machine is said to have passed the test. The test results do not depend on the machine's ability to give correct answers to questions, only how closely its answers resemble those a human would give.

The **Loebner Prize** is an annual competition in artificial intelligence that awards prizes to the computer programs considered by the judges to be the most human-like. The format of the competition is that of a standard Turing test. In each round, a human judge simultaneously holds textual conversations with a computer program and a human being via computer. Based upon the responses, the judge must decide which is which.

The contest was launched in 1990 by Hugh Loebner in conjunction with the Cambridge Center for Behavioral Studies, Massachusetts, United States. Since 2014 it has been organized by the AISB at Bletchley Park.[2] It has also been associated with Flinders University, Dartmouth College, the Science Museum in London, University of Reading and Ulster University, Magee Campus, Derry, UK City of Culture. In 2004 and 2005, it was held in Loebner's apartment in New York City. Within the field of artificial intelligence, the Loebner Prize is somewhat controversial; the most prominent critic, Marvin Minsky, called it a publicity stunt that does not help the field along.

Originally, $2,000 was awarded for the most human-seeming program in the competition. The prize was $3,000 in 2005 and $2,250 in 2006. In 2008, $3,000 was awarded.

In addition, there are two one-time-only prizes that have never been awarded. $25,000 is offered for the first program that judges cannot distinguish from a real human and which can convince judges that the human is the computer program. $100,000 is the reward for the first program that judges cannot distinguish from a real human in a Turing test that includes deciphering and understanding text, visual, and auditory input. Once this is achieved, the annual competition will end.

Supercomputer

The performance of a supercomputer is commonly measured in floating-point operations per second (FLOPS) instead of million instructions per second (MIPS). Since 2017, there are supercomputers which can perform up to nearly a hundred quadrillion FLOPS. Additional research is being conducted in China, the United States, the European Union, Taiwan and Japan to build even faster, more powerful and more technologically superior exascale supercomputers.

Supercomputers play an important role in the field of computational science, and are used for a wide range of computationally intensive tasks in various fields, including quantum mechanics, weather forecasting, climate research, oil and gas exploration, molecular modeling and physical simulations (such as simulations of the early moments of the universe, airplane and spacecraft aerodynamics, the detonation of nuclear weapons, and nuclear fusion)

The fastest supercomputer on the TOP500 supercomputer list is the Summit, in the United States, with a LINPACK benchmark score of 143.5 PFLOPS, followed by, Sierra, by around 48.860 PFLOPS. The US has five of the top 10 and China has two. In June 2018, all supercomputers on the list combined have broken the 1 exabyte mark.

A number of "special-purpose" systems have been designed, dedicated to a single problem. This allows the use of specially programmed FPGA chips or even custom ASICs, allowing better price/performance ratios by sacrificing generality. Examples of special-purpose supercomputers include Belle, Deep Blue, and Hydra, for playing chess, Gravity Pipe for astrophysics, MDGRAPE-3 for protein structure computation molecular dynamics and Deep Crack, for breaking the DES cipher.

The IBM Blue Gene/P supercomputer "Intrepid" at Argonne National Laboratory runs 164,000 processor cores using normal data center air conditioning, grouped in 40 racks/cabinets connected by a high-speed 3-D torus network.

In the 2010s, China, the United States, the European Union, and others competed to be the first to create a 1 exaFLOP (10^{18} or one quintillion FLOPS) supercomputer. Erik P. DeBenedictis of Sandia National Laboratories has theorized that a zettaFLOPS (10^{21} or one sextillion FLOPS) computer is required to accomplish full weather modeling, which could cover a two-week time span accurately. Such systems might be built around 2030.

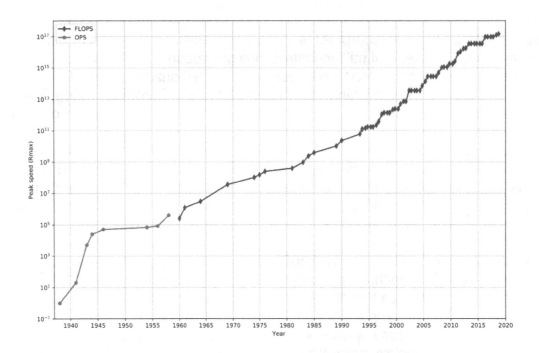

Top supercomputer speeds: *logscale speed* over 60 years.

Top 4 Supercomputers in the World, as of June 2014

Year	Supercomputer	Peak speed (Rmax)	Location
2018	IBM Summit	122.3 PFLOPS	Oak Ridge, U.S.
2016	Sunway TaihuLight	93.01 PFLOPS	Wuxi, China
2013	NUDT Tianhe-2	33.86 PFLOPS	Guangzhou, China
2012	Cray Titan	17.59 PFLOPS	Oak Ridge, U.S.

In computing, **memory** refers to the computer hardware integrated circuits that store information for immediate use in a computer; it is synonymous with the term "primary storage". Computer memory operates at a high speed, for example **random-access memory** (RAM), as a distinction from **storage** that provides slow-to-access **information** but offers higher capacities. If needed, contents of the computer memory can be transferred to **secondary storage**; a very common way of doing this is through a memory management technique called "virtual memory".

Typical secondary storage devices are **hard disk drives** and **solid-state drives**.

Flash memory

More recent flash drives (as of 2012) have much greater capacities, holding 64, 128, and 256 GB.[86]

A joint development at Intel and Micron will allow the production of 32-layer 3.5 terabyte (TB) NAND flash sticks and 10 TB standard-sized SSDs. The device includes 5 packages of 16 × 48 GB TLC dies, using a floating gate cell design.

Flash chips continue to be manufactured with capacities under or around 1 MB, e.g., for BIOS-ROMs and embedded applications.

In July 2016, Samsung announced the 4TB Samsung 850 EVO which utilizes their 256 Gb 48-layer TLC 3D V-NAND. In August 2016, Samsung announced a 32 TB 2.5-inch SAS SSD based on their 512 Gb 64-layer TLC 3D V-NAND. Further, Samsung expects to unveil SSDs with up to 100 TB of storage by 2020.

As of 2012, there are attempts to use flash memory as the main computer memory, DRAM.

It is unclear how long flash memory will persist under archival conditions – i.e., benign temperature and humidity with infrequent access with or without prophylactic rewrite. Datasheets of Atmel's flash-based "ATmega" microcontrollers typically promise retention times of 20 years at 85 °C (185 °F) and 100 years at 25 °C (77 °F).

An article from CMU in 2015 writes that "Today's flash devices, which do not require flash refresh, have a typical retention age of 1 year at room temperature." And that temperature can lower the retention time exponentially. The phenomenon can be modeled by the Arrhenius equation.

Some FPGAs are based on flash configuration cells that are used directly as (programmable) switches to connect internal elements together, using the same kind of floating-gate transistor as the flash data storage cells in data storage devices.

Robot

A **robot** is a machine—especially one programmable by a computer— capable of carrying out a complex series of actions automatically. Robots can be guided by an external control device or the control may be embedded within. Robots may be constructed on the lines of human form, but most robots are machines designed to perform a task with no regard to how they look.

Robots can be autonomous or semi-autonomous and range from humanoids such as Honda's *Advanced Step in Innovative Mobility* (ASIMO) and TOSY's *TOSY Ping Pong Playing Robot* (TOPIO) to industrial robots, medical operating robots, patient assist robots, dog therapy robots, collectively programmed *swarm* robots, UAV drones such as General Atomics MQ-1 Predator, and even microscopic nano robots. By mimicking a lifelike appearance or automating movements, a robot may convey a sense of intelligence or thought of its own. Autonomous_things are expected to proliferate in the coming decade, with home robotics and the autonomous_car as some of the main drivers. The quadrupedal military robot Cheetah, an evolution of BigDog, was clocked as the world's fastest legged robot in 2012, beating the record set by an MIT bipedal robot in 1989.

Robots have replaced humans in performing repetitive and dangerous tasks which humans prefer not to do, or are unable to do because of size limitations, or which take place in extreme environments such as outer space or the bottom of the sea. There are concerns about the increasing use of robots and their role in society. Robots are blamed for rising **technological unemployment** as they replace workers in increasing numbers of functions. The use of robots in military combat raises ethical concerns. The possibilities of robot autonomy and potential repercussions have been addressed in fiction and may be a realistic concern in the future.

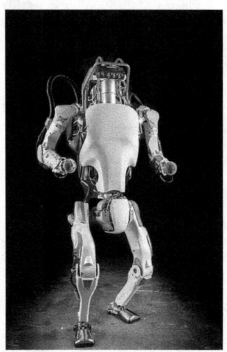 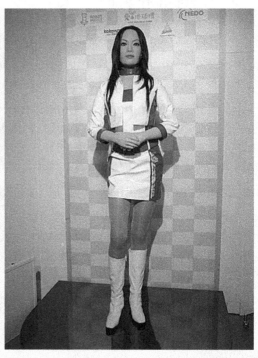

Left: Atlas (2016), a bipedal humanoid robot.
Right:_ An android, or robot designed to resemble a human, can appear comforting to some people and disturbing to others.

An **android** is a **robot** or other artificial being designed to resemble a **human**, and often made from a flesh-like material. Historically, androids were completely within the domain of **science fiction** and frequently seen in film and television, but recent advances in **robot technology** now allow the design of functional and realistic **humanoid robots**.

A **humanoid robot** is a **robot** with its body shape built to resemble the **human body**. The design may be for functional purposes, such as interacting with human tools and environments, for experimental purposes, such as the study of **bipedal locomotion**, or for other purposes. In general, humanoid robots have a torso, a head, two arms, and two legs, though some forms of humanoid robots may model only part of the body, for example, from the waist up. Some humanoid robots also have heads designed to replicate human facial features such as eyes and mouths. **Androids** are humanoid robots built to aesthetically resemble humans.

Table of current robots with 2011

2011	In November Honda unveiled its second-generation Honda **Asimo** Robot. The all new Asimo is the first version of the robot with semi-autonomous capabilities.

2012	In April, the Advanced Robotics Department in Italian Institute of Technology released its first version of the *COmpliant huMANoid* robot COMAN which is designed for robust dynamic walking and balancing in rough terrain.
2013	On December 20–21, 2013 DARPA Robotics Challenge ranked the top 16 humanoid robots competing for the US$2 million cash prize. The leading team, SCHAFT, with 27 out of a possible score of 30 was bought by Google. PAL Robotics launches REEM-C the first humanoid biped robot developed as a robotics research platform 100% ROS based.
2014	Manav – India's first 3D printed humanoid robot developed in the laboratory of A-SET Training and Research Institutes by Diwakar Vaish (head Robotics and Research, A-SET Training and Research Institutes).
2014	After the acquisition of Aldebaran, SoftBank Robotics releases the Pepper robot available for everyone.
2015	Nadine is a female humanoid social robot designed in Nanyang Technological University, Singapore, and modelled on its director Professor Nadia Magnenat Thalmann. Nadine is a socially intelligent robot which returns greetings, makes eye contact, and remembers all the conversations it has had.
2015	Sophia is a humanoid robot developed by "Hanson Robotics", Hong Kong, and modelled after Audrey Hepburn. Sophia has artificial intelligence, visual data processing and facial recognition.
2016	OceanOne, developed by a team at Stanford University, led by computer science professor Oussama Khatib, completes its first mission, diving for treasure in a shipwreck off the coast of France, at a depth of 100 meters. The robot is controlled remotely, has haptic sensors in its hands, and artificial intelligence capabilities.
2017	PAL Robotics launches TALOS, a fully electrical humanoid robot with joint torque sensors and EtherCAT communication technology that can manipulate up to 6Kg payload in each of its grippers.

Robot rights

If a machine can be created that has intelligence, could it also *feel*? If it can feel, does it have the same rights as a human? This issue, now known as "robot rights", is currently being considered by, for example, California's Institute for the Future, although many critics believe that the discussion is premature. Some critics of transhumanism argue that any hypothetical robot rights would lie on a spectrum with animal rights and human rights. The subject is profoundly discussed in the 2010 documentary film *Plug & Pray*.

Personal Computer

A **personal computer** (**PC**) is a multi-purpose computer whose capabilities, size, and price make it feasible for individual use. Personal computers are intended to be operated directly by an end user.

Since the early 1990s, Microsoft operating systems and Intel hardware have dominated much of the personal computer market, first with MS-DOS and then with Windows. Advanced Micro Devices (AMD) provides the main alternative to Intel's processors.

The advent of personal computers and the concurrent Digital Revolution have significantly affected the lives of people in all countries.

A **laptop** computer is designed, where the keyboard and computer components are on one panel, with a hinged second panel containing a flat display screen. To save weight, power and space, laptop graphics cards are in many cases integrated into the CPU or chipset and use system RAM, resulting in reduced graphics performance.

Smartphones are often similar to **tablet computers**, the difference being that smartphones always have cellular integration. They are generally smaller than tablets, and may not have a slate form factor. A tablet uses a touchscreen display, which can be controlled using either a stylus pen or finger.

The **ultra-mobile PC** (UMP) is a small tablet computer. It was developed by Microsoft, Intel and Samsung, among others. Current UMPCs typically feature the low-voltage Intel Atom or VIA C7-M processors.

A **USB flash drive**, also known as a thumb drive, pen drive, gig stick, flash stick, jump drive, disk key, disk on key (after the original M-Systems DiskOnKey drive from 2000), flash-drive, memory stick, USB key, USB stick or USB memory, is a data storage device that includes flash memory with an integrated USB interface. Most weigh less than 1 oz (28 grams).

As of March 2016, flash drives with anywhere from 8 to 256 GB were frequently sold, while 512 GB and 1 TB units were less frequent. As of 2018, 2TB flash drives were the largest available in terms of storage capacity. Some allow up to 100,000 write/erase cycles, depending on the exact type of memory chip used, and are thought to last between 10 and 100 years under normal circumstances.

USB flash drives are often used for storage, data back-up and transfer of computer files. Compared with floppy disks or CDs, they are faster, smaller, have significantly more capacity, and are more durable.

USB flash drives use the USB mass storage device class standard, supported natively by modern operating systems such as Windows, macOS, Linux, and other, as well as many BIOS boot ROMs.

Flash drive capacities on the market increase continually. High speed has become a standard for modern flash drives. Capacities exceeding 256 GB were available.

A **central processing unit** (CPU), also called a **central processor** or **main processor**, is the electronic circuitry within a computer that carries out the instructions of a computer program by performing the basic arithmetic, logic, controlling, and input/output (I/O) operations specified by the instructions.

Back cover:

Book is described the arrangement of the Universe. This is the scientific prediction of the non-biological (electronic) civilization and immortality of human being. Such a prognosis is predicated upon a new law, discovered by the author, for the development of complex systems. According to this law, every self-copying system tends to be more complex than the previous system, provided that all external conditions remain the same. The consequences are disastrous: humanity will be replaced by a new civilization created by intellectual robots (which the author refers to as "E-humans" and "E-beings"), These creatures, whose intellectual and mechanical abilities will far exceed those of man, will require neither food nor oxygen to sustain their existence. They may have the emotion. Capable of developing science, technology and their own intellectual abilities thousands of times faster than humans can, they will, in essence, be eternal.

About the Authors

Alexander A. Bolonkin was born in former USSR. He holds a doctoral degree in Aviation Engineering from Moscow Aviation Institute and a post-doctoral degree in Aerospace Engineering from Leningrad Polytechnic University. He has held the positions senior engineer at the Antonov Aircraft Design Company and chairman of the Reliability Department at the Glushko Rocket Design Company. He has also lectured at the Moscow Aviation Universities. Following his arrival in the USA in 1988, he lectured at the New Jersey Institute of Technology and worked as a senior researcher at NASA and the US Air Force Research Laboratories.

Professor Bolonkin is the author of more than 270 scientific articles and books, and 17 inventions to his credit. His most notable books include: The Development of Soviet Rocket Engines (Delphic Ass., Inc., Washington , 1991); Non-Rocket Space Launch and Flight, (Elsevier, 2005); New Concepts, Ideas, Innovation in Aerospace, Technology and Human Life (NOVA, 2006); Macro-Projects: Environment and Technology (NOVA, 2007), "New Technologies and Revolutionary Projects", Scribd, 2009, 324 pgs.

www.ingramcontent.com/pod-product-compliance
Lightning Source LLC
Chambersburg PA
CBHW060504060326
40689CB00020B/4629